The
Teenager
Manual

Published in June 2007

British Library Cataloguing in Publication Data:
A catalogue record for this book is available
from the British Library

ISBN 978 1 84425 409 5

Published by Haynes Publishing, Sparkford, Yeovil,
Somerset BA22 7JJ, UK
Tel: 01963 442030 Fax: 01963 440001
Int. tel: +44 1963 442030 Int. fax: +44 1963 440001
E-mail: sales@haynes.co.uk
Website: www.haynes.co.uk

Haynes North America Inc.
861 Lawrence Drive, Newbury Park, California 91320, USA

Printed and bound in Great Britain
by J. H. Haynes & Co. Ltd, Sparkford

The
Teenager
Manual

Practical advice for all parents

Dr Pat Spungin

Haynes Publishing

Contents

Contents

Introduction

Teenagers are often compared with toddlers; both are intent on asserting themselves, predisposed to say 'No', prone to tantrums if crossed, eager to explore the world, and often careless of their own safety in doing so. Parents of toddlers will find many books, television programmes and magazine articles to help them cope, but unfortunately there is less help for the parents of teenagers, and their need is often greater. When things go wrong between parent and teenager, they can go seriously wrong. The majority of calls to parent helpline ParentlinePlus concern problems with teenagers, and a large proportion of the requests for help on my own website, **www.raisingkids.co.uk**, are likewise from the distraught parents of teens.

Nothing that precedes the onset of adolescence prepares you for dealing with the process of moving from dependent, loving and accepting child to stroppy know-it-all teenager. Having had three teenagers myself I know that the issues parents face can vary from child to child, but some concerns are common to all parents of teens. How to talk to them about puberty, sex and relationships? How much freedom to give and when? How to make sure that school work doesn't suffer as the attractions of the peer group and its culture take over? What to say about underage drinking and smoking? And most important, how to deal with all these issues while remaining on good terms?

Though apparently eager to break free of the family, teens still need the support and guidance of their parents. My aims in this manual are to help parents adapt to the changes their children are undergoing, and to keep their family relationships strong while at the same time allowing their children more freedom to learn for themselves.

A final word: if you are the parent of a ten or eleven-year-old, now is the time to think about their teen years. As children 'grow older younger', so the teen years often start well before a child reaches thirteen. Be prepared.

Dr Pat Spungin, 2007

> *Adolescence is a period of rapid changes. Between the ages of 12 and 17, for example, a parent ages as much as 20 years.*
> **Anon**

Chapter 1

What parents can expect

1 Introduction

Adolescence is a time of transition and, like all changes, needs careful handling. Both parents and children have mixed feelings about what is happening. Parents want to hang on to childhood and, at the same time, look forward to their children growing into independent and responsible young people who can successfully manage their own lives. Children want to rush into the excitement of adult life and they often want to do it when (in their parents' eyes) they are too young and too immature to handle the challenges.

Growing from dependent child to independent, self-sufficient adult is a confusing and difficult process. Teenagers and toddlers are similar in more respects than you might think:

- ☐ They want to be more independent
- ☐ They want to assert themselves
- ☐ They don't have enough experience to understand potential risks
- ☐ They're undergoing big physical and emotional changes
- ☐ When crossed they're likely to throw a tantrum

Learning to walk before you run

Toddlers learning to walk will first hold on until they feel steady enough to let go, then they'll take one step alone, then several, and so in time they learn to walk without effort. Eventually, they are able to run.

Psychologically speaking, the process of becoming an independent adult is not dissimilar. Progressively, parents let go and young people become more and more independent and self-sufficient. Problems arise when teenagers literally want to run before they can walk and parents, fearing that they will fall, are reluctant to let go.

2 Understanding what teenagers want

Trying to negotiate the choppy waters of adolescence is difficult for parents. They are used to making all the critical decisions in their child's life. They expect to be listened to and for their views to be accepted without arguement. Then adolescence changes everything.

Teenagers are constantly pushing the boundaries, wanting more independence and freedom to make their own choices. They no longer accept their parents' views blindly. After all, most parents know little about the things that are important to their teens, like music, popular culture and even schoolwork.

There is no 'naughty step' for teenagers

The options available to parents to discipline their teens are limited. To effectively manage the transition from child to adult with a minimum of upset, parents have to modify their own behaviour and change their approach to parenting.

Key issues for teenagers

■ Freedom

Throughout the teenage years, there is a push for increasing freedom to explore life, friendships and other experiences without parental interference. The issue of how much freedom to give, and when, is one of the major flashpoints between the generations.

■ Friendship

Friendships and peer groups become more important than ever in the lives of young people. Teens choose a peer group which shares their experiences, attitudes and values. There is a multiplicity of teenage tribes, with constantly changing names, all linked by music, each tribe believing itself to be the only group that is not a slavish follower of fashion. The peer group (the gang) become the most important social group in the lives of teenagers whose home life is emotionally impoverished, and who feel little connection with their family. If the peer group does something that goes against the family values, teens may choose the gang standpoint over that of the family.

■ Identity

Part of becoming an adult is developing personal identity, values and beliefs. Often teenagers do this is in opposition to what their parents stand for – solidly middle-class parents can be outraged by unconventional tastes in dress and music, or religious offspring can cause incomprehension in an atheist family.

■ Meaning

As teenagers grow they begin to think about the wider world and important moral and ethical issues. Many young people look for a cause or commitment that is 'bigger' than themselves to which they can give allegiance. Religion, politics, environmental issues, and animal rights are all part of the search for meaning and significance in life.

■ Respect

Teens want to feel respected and valued for their choices, and not be criticised for their appearance, music, friends and schoolwork. When parents disparage their lifestyle, the reaction of a typical teenager is: 'You don't have to like my choice but give me some respect and don't criticise it.' A good rule of thumb is not to pass the kind of personal remarks about your children that you wouldn't pass about your friends.

■ Responsibility

As pre-teens become teens, they have more responsibility. This begins with issues as trivial as travelling on public transport to a new school and ends with being able to organise themselves to find work or win a place in higher education.

■ Security

Just because teens seem to be struggling to break free from parental control doesn't mean they don't need their family. Young people want to feel safe and secure, physically and emotionally. They want reliable and trustworthy adults in their lives to whom they can turn for advice and support. Research shows that teenagers who are loved and supported at home are more likely to make sensible choices in the outside world.

3 What concerns parents

■ Safety
Parents want their children to be safe in what they may see as a dangerous world. They know that many teens are risk-takers who want to have 'adult' experiences. Parents fear their teenagers may smoke, indulge in underage drinking, be offered drugs and have sexual encounters which they are too young to manage. It is this concern for their teenager's safety that leads parents to restrict their independence and freedom, especially under the age of 16.

■ Home or hotel?
It appears to parents that their children are never home and that family life is less important, even unimportant, to them. When they are home they shut themselves in their bedrooms, are reluctant to be physically affectionate, and don't ask for help and advice as they used to. Consequently parents feel powerless, rejected and sometimes angry.

■ Loss of control
A teenager's freedom is a parent's loss of control. For some parents it feels as if they have lost the ability to influence their child's future. On the other hand, adolescents feel they are controlled too much, and want to have more choice. A fully-functioning adult needs to make responsible choices, so the journey through adolescence to adulthood requires that parents grant their children the freedom to learn from experience, exercise choice and take on responsibilities. This includes the freedom to make mistakes.

■ Identity and identification
Parents can see children as an extension of themselves. When they look at their offspring they identify with what they see. They are proud of their children for their talents and achievements. When parents don't like what they see of their teen's behaviour and appearance, they show their disapproval. They pass remarks about clothing, friends, music and much more. But times are changing. Children who were once prepared to defer to adult taste and opinions now have tastes and opinions of their own, and they don't like to have them criticised. They will undoubtedly tell you that 'other people's parents let them' and 'everyone is going' and that may be correct.

4 Letting go

As adolescent children become more assertive and confrontational, the tendency of some parents is to increase their own force to meet them head on. This doesn't really help, especially with spirited children who will fight their own corner and in some cases simply refuse to comply. The disciplinary options are limited. Parents cannot physically restrain a teenager. They can limit their privileges and remove mobile phones or computer access, they can stop any pocket money or allowance, but if the teenager is prepared to tough it out there is not a lot parents can do.

Parents are often slow to recognise what 'letting go' means in the teenage years. When teenagers start to think and choose for themselves, that's when the arguments begin. The time for telling is over and the time for talking and discussion has arrived.

Sooner or later your teenager will have to go it alone

It's possible to keep a teen under your thumb for a certain amount of time, but the time will come when they will do their own thing – behind their parents' backs. Eventually, teenagers will leave home. At that point parents can't stop their child taking a wrong decision or hanging out with friends they dislike. All they can hope for is that during adolescence their teenagers have learned how to take care of themselves and make sensible, healthy decisions.

Signs of Growing Independence

Anticipate the changes. The changes during adolescence are not only physical. Signs that your teenager is becoming more independent include:

- Wanting to spend leisure time with friends not family
- Wanting to make trips on their own to the shops or cinema
- Developing views and opinions of their own
- Answering back

- Moodiness and unpredictability
- Retreating to their room to spend hours texting or on he computer.
- Wanting more fashionable clothing
- Asking for money to buy music magazines, computer games and so on

Recognise that the world has changed

When dealing with teenagers many parents look back to their own teenage years. They remember their own experiences, such as going to places that were potentially dangerous, accepting lifts from drivers who had drunk too much, experimenting with drugs/drink and sexual experiences they were too young for. Now, as parents, they worry that their own teenagers will also do these things.

Children today push for greater freedom at a younger age. Perhaps you were 16 before you went inside a pub or went to an all-night party, but today your 14-year-old may be asking for the same privileges. Nevertheless, if they really *are* too young to handle it then stick to your guns and don't give in just because everyone else does!

Have faith in the work you've done to date

Contrary to media hype, most teenagers pass through their teenage years relatively trouble-free. Recent research has shown that nearly 60 per cent of young people say they 'get on well with their parents', and a survey in 2000 revealed that the person the majority of teenagers most admire is their mother.

When you are teaching a child to ride a bicycle the time eventually comes to let go of the saddle, even if the child might fall off and hurt itself. Similarly, as a parent of a teen the time comes to let go and take the risk that the teenager will make a mistake. Experience is the best teacher. All of us learn from the consequences of our decisions. What young people need is someone who believes in them enough to trust them and let them go.

> It's better to give privileges slowly. You'll find it much easier to allow more freedom gradually than to rein it in when you feel things have gone too far.

When you feel the urge to pass a critical comment:

☐ Imagine they are someone else's teenager;
☐ Ask yourself 'would I still be critical if it wasn't my son or daughter...?
☐ ...and if the answer is 'no'... then don't say it!

Show respect

'Letting go' means parents also have to let go of any preconceived ideas they might have had of what their child would become. It's important to accept teens for what they are. They are themselves, which may be completely different from what their parents expected or wanted. They are not an extension of their parents. A piece of good advice for parents is not to try to change them into something different. Accept and respect what they are becoming and help them become the best they can be.

Let them make mistakes

If children are brought up to think for themselves and show initiative, at some point they will think and do things their parents don't like. Now the parents' hidden agenda becomes clear. Summed up it is, 'Yes, think for yourself – but think the same things I do.' Teens are entitled to their views and as long as they aren't doing anything harmful to themselves or others they should be allowed to make their own decisions, even if, in their parents' view, they are wrong.

Provide backup

Letting go isn't an 'all or nothing' situation. At the beginning parents can let go and yet still provide some support. When teenagers start to travel to school on public transport they are often given a mobile phone as an additional support. If you have agreed to your teenager staying out late, you can still collect them so that they do not have to come home alone. Parents who worry about the company their teen is keeping can invite their friends into the house, to see what they are really like.

5 How to be a successful parent of a teenager

Be prepared

Watch for the onset of adolescence in a pre-teen – many young people show adolescent behaviour before they turn 13. They may become more moody and emotional, and also surly, rude and inconsiderate. Be sympathetic with the moods and be prepared to make some concessions as they get older; but don't accept rudeness and surliness and lack of respect. Bad behaviour from your 10 or 11-year-old will only get worse if you let it pass. The first time your pre-teen or teen calls you a name or tells you where to go, make it absolutely clear that this kind of behaviour is not acceptable.

Know what's really important

If parents have a clear idea of what is really important for their adolescent they will know where to make a stand and where to give in. Four areas in particular are important during the teenage years:

■ Education

School, and academic achievement, is important.

This doesn't necessarily mean gaining entry to a top university, but every teenager should apply themselves enough at school to realise their potential. If doing well at school is a priority, this will impact on a number of other decisions about:

♦ *Sleep*
It's essential that teens get enough sleep to perform well the following day at school. Among other things this means that children are not allowed out late on a school night.

♦ *Distractions*
Computers and television in the bedroom distract teenagers from doing their homework.

♦ *Friendships*
Be wary of friends who are disruptive in school or are anti-education.

♦ *Behaviour*
Young people need to develop good habits, like getting up on time, putting in the time and effort to pass exams, and being organised about homework and other school commitments.

■ **Harmful behaviour**
Parents want to be sure that their teenager won't follow the peer group blindly into drinking, drug use and precocious sex. This is a question of judging the maturity of the teen, and their self-confidence and self-respect. The questions a parent needs to ask cover things like:

♦ *'Is my child mature enough and confident enough to say 'no' when faced with a potentially dangerous situation?*
The answer is not related to age but will vary between teenagers. Teenagers who feel valued for themselves and have a strong home life are less likely to be involved in harmful activities.

♦ *'Am I confident of the values she/he has learned at home, like sensible attitudes to alcohol, and respect for their body and health?'*

Most of these values are developed in the growing child but they are often tested in the maturing adolescent. Unfortunately, this doesn't mean they will never drink too much or try cigarettes, but their behaviour is unlikely to spiral out of control.

■ Self-respect

It's important for most parents that their teenagers should grow into confident and mature individuals. Confidence comes with being given more responsibility, within limits. Areas in which responsibility can be given during teenage years include:

♦ *Managing money*
  Don't make everything too easy for them by doling out money regardless. Encourage them to work for their extra cash, even if it only involves jobs in the house.

♦ *Managing themselves*
  Occasionally ask yourself questions such as, 'Should I still be waking my teenager at 16 or should they be able to get themselves up in the morning?'

♦ *Household*
  Encourage them to learn to cook for themselves, to keep their room tidy and to help with the household chores. In my opinion, there is no reason why anyone over the age of 15 should not do their own washing.

■ Respect for other people

Teenagers sensing their growing independence from the family sometimes react by being aggressive and rude to their parents and to other members of the family. They may bully younger siblings, intimidate their parents, or refuse to get involved with family activities. Being a teenager is not an excuse for bad behaviour. Once they start to behave in a disrespectful way it's time to make it clear that such behaviour is not acceptable and that, if it continues, there will be adverse consequences.

> **NOTE**
> It may seem in this book that parents are asked to make all the compromises. This is not the case. My view is that their position is stronger if they are prepared to concede on things that are important to the teenager but not important to them. On matters that are important to the teen's wellbeing, parents should *not* compromise but should stand firm.
>
> I also believe that it is very difficult to change a teenager's behaviour by force. Much of what is recommended in this manual is based on the assumption that if parents modify their own behaviour they will see a change in their teenager's behaviour in response. This change is not always immediate, but over time it will be effective.

Know what's not really important

This includes superficial things like music, appearance, and the culture of the peer group – as long as it doesn't work against the things that parents value.

And finally...

Most teens grow out of adolescent moodiness and emotionality and mature into sensible adults. They often look back on their time as a teenager and regret the distress they caused to their parents. They may even come to realise that their parents were right and they were wrong at the time.

> '*When I was a boy of fourteen, my father was so ignorant I could hardly stand to have the old man around. But when I got to be twenty-one, I was astonished at how much he had learned.*'
>
> **Mark Twain**

> Don't wait for bad behaviour to become a habit. At the first sign, tell your teenager that speaking/behaving in such a way is not allowed.

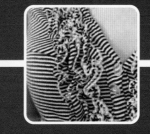

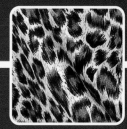

Chapter 2

Your adolescent's physical development

1 Introduction

As their bodies begin to change, it's important that youngsters know what to expect. Don't assume that they have already learned everything in the classroom. They may have learned much of it in the playground, in which case they will definitely need accurate and reliable information.

Getting that information across will not always be easy. Adolescence is a time of confusion, self-consciousness and mixed feelings about physical developments. Many boys won't want to talk to their mothers nor girls to their fathers. Some won't want to talk to either, in which case a good book on the subject, which they can read in private, will be invaluable (see the appendix for suitable teen-friendly books).

Teens need to know what will happen to their bodies during puberty, how they will change, and what is 'normal'. If you're wondering when to start a discussion about forthcoming developments, keep an eye on your child's friends, as their development will alert you to what will soon happen to your own son or daughter. These changes usually start earlier for girls than for boys.

2 Your teenage girl's developing body

In Britain, the average age for the onset of puberty among girls is 11. Some girls may begin to develop as early as 8 and others may show no obvious changes until 15–16. By 13, some girls are almost physically mature, but there are wide variations in the ages when puberty begins and ends. Girls tend to take after their mothers in the age of onset.

How girls develop
☐ A growth spurt around the age of 9 or 10
☐ Initial breast budding at 9–11 years
☐ Oilier skin and hair at 10–12 years
☐ Developing sweat glands and a more 'adult' body odour at 10–12 years
☐ Light pubic and underarm hair at 11–13 years
☐ Vaginal discharge usually starts a few months before the first period
☐ The beginning of menstruation at 12–13 years
☐ Pubic and underarm hair becoming thicker and a more curvy, womanly figure developing gradually as your daughter grows

Puberty is a time of conflicting emotions; excitement at growing up and becoming a woman, and at the same time fear and anxiety about leaving the security of childhood. Many of these conflicting emotions centre on what is happening to the girl's body. Girls who are physically advanced for their age will be embarrassed about their fuller body, breast development and starting their periods. They may be teased in school, especially by the boys. Girls who are late developers fear they will never develop and feel like children alongside their more developed friends.

Breast development
Breast development is usually the first sign of puberty. Many girls are surprised when the breast 'buds' start swelling and some find developing breasts tender or painful at times. When breast development starts, explain that this is normal and not a sign that something is wrong. Tenderness shouldn't last more than a couple of

months, although it might return for a short time with another spurt in breast growth. If she feels really sore, Calpol can help.

If sore breasts are a serious problem, consider a support bra for activities like gym – most department stores have Lycra sports bras in small sizes, which look like vests rather than lingerie. If she has severe, acute pain rather than aching and tenderness, long-term pain or pain that centres on an unusual lump, ask your doctor's advice.

After initial breast budding, breasts will gradually begin to swell, though it'll take a while before they grow big enough to need a bra. This too can be a little painful and a well-fitting, supportive bra will help. Many girls look forward to their first bra and want something that is pretty but not necessarily supportive. Bras that are a mix of pretty and practical are a good idea at this stage. At first you may have to go shopping every couple of months as cup sizes change rapidly. Breasts usually enlarge and develop at the same rate but sometimes one grows faster than the other. This is nothing to worry about.

Other changes
At the time her breasts begin to grow, your daughter may be taller than most of the boys in her class! The majority of a girl's growth will be almost complete by her 13th birthday.

As puberty progresses, a girl's pubic hair begins to grow, darken, and become curlier, and her body will become more rounded, developing the curves of womanhood.

Changes in body shape, odour, and possibly acne as a result of oilier skin, can make girls feel self-conscious. Be reassuring and be ready to provide practical help in the form of toiletries and skincare products.

Menstruation
As girls approach their teen years, changes occur to prepare the body for pregnancy. Once the body, brain and womb are mature enough, a monthly bleeding cycle occurs. The lining of the womb prepares for pregnancy each month. If a

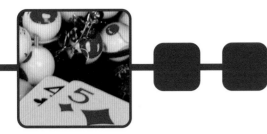

pregnancy does not occur, the lining is washed clean with blood. This blood appears from the vagina. This monthly cycle is called menstruation, usually referred to as her 'period'.

When will it start?

A generation ago it was unusual for girls to begin menstruating before they reached their teens, but today it is not unlikely that the first period will occur while she's still at primary school. Though girls start menstruating at the average age of 12 they can begin as early as 8 years of age or as late as 16. If menstruation has not started by age 16, seek professional help. There are tests that can check for normal growth and cycles.

Although there's no 'right' age for a girl to get her period, there are some clues that menstruation will start soon. Typically, a girl gets her period 18 months to two years after her breasts start to develop. Height is another clue. Most girls have almost reached their adult height when they get their first period. They rarely grow more than an inch or two (50mm) after they begin menstruating.

Menstruation is usually preceded by a vaginal discharge, which is clear or whitish a couple of months before her period begins. If she's aware of this, her first period will be less unexpected.

The cycle

The average menstrual cycle lasts 28–30 days but varies from individual to individual, with some as short as 22 days and others as long as 35. Typically, a period lasts between five and seven days but again there is

considerable variation. Once periods start it may take the body time to adjust, and in the first year or two periods are often irregular.

Pre-menstrual problems

Some girls have hardly any problems with menstruation but others have symptoms ranging from feeling bloated to severe pain. Other common symptoms include:

☐ Aggression and irritability
☐ Cramps
☐ Food cravings
☐ Headaches
☐ Loss of concentration
☐ Mood swings
☐ Tender breasts
☐ Tiredness

If these symptoms are severe they may be a sign of Pre Menstrual Syndrome (PMS). Although this is most common in women over 30, some teens do suffer from it. PMS can occur for up to two weeks prior to a period but disappears once the period starts.

For cramps and minor pain, take over-the-counter medications like paracetamol. Alternative ways of treating period pain include:

☐ A hot water bottle held on the abdomen
☐ Avoiding foods with caffeine, sugar or salt
☐ Meditation or relaxation
☐ Regular exercise

It takes about a year for the menstrual cycle to become established. Once it has settled, there are some changes that should be referred to your GP if they occur:

☐ A missed period
☐ An unusual amount of pain before or during periods
☐ Bleeding between periods
☐ Periods that are heavier than usual
☐ Periods that last longer than a week

3 Practical preparation: your daughter

Try to anticipate your daughter's needs. A box of pads in the bathroom (that she can help herself from) will be appreciated, though girls who feel shy about their puberty may prefer not to have pads in such a public place. Your daughter will let you know what is best for her.

Talking to the school

Is it a good idea to contact the primary school if your daughter is an early starter? Yes; she won't be the only girl who has started but it is possible her primary school won't have dispensers or even disposal bins. The school is obliged to provide soap, loo paper and whatever is necessary for hygiene, so they should install disposal bins if they are needed. Sanitary towels are available in the majority of schools, although most girls will have to ask an adult.

Discuss the situation with a sympathetic woman teacher, to whom your daughter can go if she is 'caught short' at school or if she has pain or discomfort. Make sure she always has enough sanitary protection on hand – cycles can be very unpredictable, especially in the first year. The same goes for painkillers – your GP can advise on the best brands that are safe for under-13s.

It's common for secondary school children to carry their schoolbags with them as they change rooms according to their timetable, but primary school children tend to stay in the same classroom for the majority of the time and hang their bags in the cloakroom. This makes it harder for young girls to discretely carry their 'period kit', especially as they usually prefer to use pads at the beginning. Make sure she has a discrete container.

There is a wide range of sanitary products available. Look for slim, high-absorbency brands which take up little space but offer enough protection. Some manufacturers make packets of wipes and disposal bags.

Pads or tampons? Tampons are less bulky, and better for sport and activities, but many young girls don't feel ready for them in the first year or two.

Tampax and Lillets both produce leaflets aimed at girls who are using tampons for the first time. For free copies, visit www.tampax.co.uk (or phone 0800 378135) or www.lil-lets.com (or phone 0121 697 3884).

However old your daughter is at the time of her first period and however well-prepared, it can sometimes make girls feel a little unsettled. Unlike boys, the first period is a definite event that marks the fact that they now have a fully-functioning woman's body. Some girls have mixed feelings about their childhood being officially 'over'.

Periods don't mean the process of puberty is completely over, but girls are usually at physical maturity by 17 and have fully developed reproductive organs. However, body hair may continue to grow and thicken for several years more, and breasts may become heavier. Slight 'chubbiness' is common and may in itself be a source of insecurity. Keep an eye on your teen's eating habits in case she begins to skip meals in an attempt to lose weight.

provide support and to answer her questions. The same friend or relative can also be called upon to help with buying bras.

As your girl matures, bear in mind that she will need more privacy, especially if she is the only female in the household. Make sure she can lock the bathroom door when she needs to, and sort out somewhere for her to store her pads or tampons away from public view. If she has brothers or younger siblings encourage them to respect her private space too, without necessarily spelling out the reasons in detail.

A few dos and don'ts

- [ ] Do prepare your daughter. If she knows what to expect she is more likely to take it in her stride.
- [ ] Do have sanitary products readily available so she doesn't need to ask.
- [ ] Do have suitable products available for spots, and a good deodorant.
- [ ] Do help her be aware of her cycle and anticipate her own needs – early periods are likely to be very irregular.
- [ ] Do make sure her clothing fits properly. Most school uniforms are sized for children and she may need more accommodating blouses that don't gape at the front.
- [ ] Don't announce it to family and friends.
- [ ] Don't tease her about mood swings, PMS and other references to her periods.

Single dads with daughters

Single fathers may be uncomfortable talking to their daughter about the way her body is changing. Try to take the lead from her – she may not find it a problem at all – and if you still feel awkward, ask a female friend or relative to

4 Your teenage boy's developing body

Eleven is the average age for boys to enter puberty, but it can occur any time between 9 and 15 years.

How boys develop
- [ ] Oilier skin and hair at 11–13 years
- [ ] Dark fluff on upper lip at 11–13 years
- [ ] Enlargement of the testes at around 11 years
- [ ] Thinning and reddening of the scrotum at around 11 years
- [ ] Developing sweat glands and a more 'adult' body odour at 11–13 years
- [ ] Pubic and underarm hair at 11–13 years
- [ ] Growth spurt (later than girls – usually a couple of years after the start of puberty)
- [ ] Penis becomes longer and broader between 13–17 years
- [ ] 'Wet dreams' and spontaneous erections become more common at 13–17 years
- [ ] Voice grows deeper and 'breaks' at 15–17 years
- [ ] Needs to shave regularly at 16–18 years

Boys run considerably behind girls in terms of physical development. By age 13, when many girls are almost physically mature, most boys are just beginning to develop. Puberty begins with a growth spurt and the boy will grow on average 4in (100mm) in a year. They also experience muscle growth and start to take on a manly physique. This growth spurt usually reaches its peak about two years after the start of puberty.

The first sign of puberty is likely to be enlargement of the testes, thinning of the scrotum and possibly a light growth of pubic hair. This often occurs at around 11 years old. Body odour may also be noticeable for the first time. Testicle and scrotum growth begins in early to mid-puberty. Penis growth starts a bit later but continues for a longer period. A penis will grow longer first, followed by overall broadening, and as development begins 'wet dreams' are likely. Now

spontaneous erections can happen at inconvenient times, causing great embarrassment.

The growth spurt may be delayed for a few boys, who are also likely to have late pubertal growth in other areas (including late penis growth). This can cause a pre-teen considerable anguish. Don't wait for your son to come to you with his worries. Embarrassment may stop him from doing so. Take the initiative and bring up the subject yourself, if he remains considerably behind his peers in development. A doctor's reassurance will help a boy understand that he will grow eventually and that many other boys are in the same situation.

Pubic and underarm hair becomes thicker as puberty progresses. Light facial hair will appear, but is unlikely to require shaving straight away. The voice may deepen and even begin to crack, and acne may develop as a result of oilier skin and hair.

Boys grow rapidly after their 15th birthday and finally begin to shoot past the girls. However, pubertal changes will continue until at least 17. Different parts of the body grow at different rates and this creates problems of coordination. Boys often look and move a little awkwardly as they try to adjust to their rapid increase in height. This gradually changes as boys become accustomed to their size and begin to look more 'manly' as their shoulders broaden and their muscles thicken all over.

Most boys' voices break by 17. The penis and testicles usually reach full adult size and sperm becomes fully mature, while body and pubic hair becomes thicker and darker and facial hair increases. By this time your son may need to shave every few days.

5 Practical preparation: your son

When the changes of puberty kick in, being a late or early developer can be tricky. In a classroom some boys will be as tall as a man, while others will still look like children. Boys become more self-conscious around girls, especially in early adolescence.

Boys' bodies undergo sudden and, sometimes, dramatic changes during puberty. As well as facial hair, voice breaking, etc, there may be swelling breast tissue and changes in the size and colour of the nipple area. This is quite normal in early puberty but teenage boys will still need to be reassured that these changes are natural and expected. A boy maybe too embarrassed to talk about the changes he is experiencing and the conflicting emotions that accompany them, so buy a book about the subject that he can read alone.

Single mums with sons

As their sons approach adolescence single mums may worry if there is no male partner or big brother

in the household. Teenage boys appreciate having the following masculine stuff available at home:

- ☐ Fragrance-free (or 'masculine' smelling) toiletries
- ☐ Facial soap and/or cleanser formulated for male skin, which is thicker, oilier and, surprisingly, more delicate than a woman's
- ☐ Disposable razors and shaving foam (an electric razor can be a thoughtful gift)
- ☐ Men's deodorant/antiperspirant

Shaving without tears

If Dad isn't around and getting help from a male relative isn't an option (or you're a mother who prefers to be the one to show her son how to shave), don't worry. This male mystery isn't rocket science.

■ Tools of the trade

- ◆ Razor (traditional or electric) and shaving cream or gel, to reduce friction and make it easier to pull the razor against the skin.
- ◆ Aftershave is optional. Strongly-perfumed aftershaves can be high in alcohol, and are too drying for young skin.
- ◆ Shaving can remove some of the skin's natural moisture, so some boys may want to use after-shave moisturiser if their skin feels dry.
- ◆ A traditional razor is much cheaper than electric, but make sure the blade is new and sharp to prevent cuts. Most boys prefer an electric razor when they first start shaving, because it lets them get a feel for it without worrying about cutting themselves. An electric razor doesn't shave as close as a traditional one but that's not a big issue for a 14-year-old!

■ Method

For the first few attempts, he should pick a time when he hasn't got anywhere to go immediately afterwards. All boys end up with a few nicks and cuts and it's best not to share their battle-scars with the world. The best time to shave is just after a shower or bath. Start by washing the face and

neck thoroughly with mild soap – the force required to cut beard hair is reduced by almost 70 per cent after a two-minute application of warm water. Then apply plenty of shaving cream or gel.

The trick is to go slowly! A boy's face has lots of curves and angles, and it's easy for him to cut himself if he rushes. Use light, gentle strokes when shaving, and rinse the razor frequently to stop hairs and shaving cream clogging up the blade edges.

Begin with the cheeks, sides of the face and the neck, and leave hard-to-shave spots for last. The toughest whiskers grow on the chin and around the lips, so more time soaking in the shaving cream will soften them further. When finished, rinse face and neck with cool water and pat dry, and then apply a little moisturising lotion. At the end of every shave rinse the blade thoroughly and shake off the excess water before putting the razor away (don't wipe the blade as it will damage the edge).

You'll need to talk about relationships, values and potential risks with your child, as well as explaining the physical changes that your child should expect during puberty. You know it's important, but many parents can find it a bit embarrassing. Our chapters on emotional issues and parenting skills are full of helpful advice for getting conversations started.

The timescale for teenagers' physical development varies a lot. However, anyone over 14 years of age who hasn't begun to develop any secondary sexual characteristics (breast swelling in girls and light pubic and underarm hair in boys) should visit their GP, who will probably recommend an appointment with an endocrinologist (hormonal specialist), to make sure there isn't a medical reason behind the delay.

6 Not just the plumbing

Has your pre-teen started spending hours in the bathroom? Or would a little more soap-and-water not go amiss? Body hair, maturing sweat glands, pimples, greasy skin and lank hair can accompany the onset of puberty, as can gaining a few extra kilos. These changes can be hard on self-esteem. A good diet and exercise will help with most of the problems. Support them by stocking up the fruit bowl and encouraging active participation in sport.

How bodily changes affect teens

■ Concern about how they are developing can affect both boys and girls

Teens will inevitably compare themselves to their peers, and being 'out of developmental step' can cause problems, as most teenagers just want to fit in and be like everyone else.

■ Early-maturing boys may be expected to behave in a more mature manner than their less developed peers

Though their bodies may resemble those of much older boys, they are not emotionally mature and may find expectations to behave in a more mature way difficult to cope with.

■ Early-maturing girls may face unwanted attention from older boys and feel unable to cope

Research shows that early-maturing girls have greater incidence of eating disorders and anxiety.

■ Late maturity may result in difficulties

Parents who may feel relieved that their children have not yet reached the turbulent adolescent years, should nevertheless recognise that late maturity can bring with it problems of its own. Late-maturing boys may feel overwhelmed by their more adult-looking peers and fear they will never fully mature.

Teens will sleep more

Research suggests that teens need more sleep while undergoing such rapid growth. On average teens need between eight and nine-and-a-half hours per night.

Teens may feel awkward about demonstrating affection to the opposite sex parent

As they develop physically, teens are beginning to rethink their interactions with the opposite sex. An adolescent girl who used to hug and kiss her dad may now shy away. A boy who used to kiss his mother good night, may now wave to her on his way up the stairs.

Eating well

Build strong bodies with a healthy diet. Attitudes to food, size and weight are learned at home, so healthy role models within the family are crucial. A parent who is constantly dieting is setting a bad example, just as anyone who makes jokes about overweight celebrities is sending a message that thinner is better. Critical comments on your own body size or the shape of others are best avoided.

As well as having a sensible attitude towards eating, what you eat at home is important. As they will probably be tempted by all kinds of junk food in the outside world, encourage your children to eat a healthy balanced diet (salads and greens as well as meat and fish) at home; but don't talk about 'good food and bad food'.

Make mealtimes together fun and relaxed

Family meals should be something to look forward to – an opportunity to catch up at the end of the day. Don't discuss problems or row at the dinner table; nothing is guaranteed to spoil the appetite faster. Research shows that eating as a family is one of the most effective ways of helping teenagers avoid getting involved in addictive behaviours and has a positive impact on school achievement.

Body image

Body image is a preoccupation of many teenagers and not only girls. Increasingly boys are also falling prey to concerns about their body image. Boys may wonder why they are not developing a masculine physique or fear they are too skinny, chubby or short compared to their peers. If your teen seems to be severely concerned with negative body image, consider making an appointment with your doctor. (Eating disorders are discussed in detail later in the book.)

7 Sleep

Typical sleep requirements of teens (and pre-teens) are:

- ☐ 11 years old – 9½ hours
- ☐ 12–13 years old – 9¼ hours
- ☐ 14 years old – 9 hours
- ☐ 15 years old – 8¾ hours
- ☐ 16 years old – 8½ hours
- ☐ 17 years old – 8 hours

At weekends, young people frequently stay up late and then sleep until noon or longer. This can have a significant impact on their sleep cycle and they may well end up being sleep-deprived during the working week, when they should be at their most alert.

The way to deal with this is to try to get teens not to stray more than a couple of hours from the boundaries of their 'normal' sleep patterns. If teens usually go to bed at 10pm, discourage them from staying up after midnight. If their usual getting up time is 7am, discourage them from sleeping past 10am at the weekend. This will not prove easy!

8 Height and weight chart

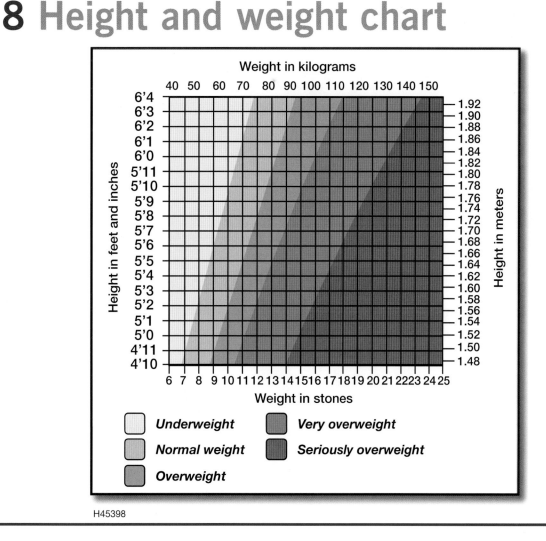

Chapter 3

Teenagers' emotions

1 Why emotions run high

Academic demands, different groups of friends, new responsibilities and expectations, and surging hormones all combine to make teenagers' lives difficult. Their bodies are experiencing drastic changes and so are their emotions.

Teenagers question everything

Very young children believe in their parents 100 per cent and can't function outside the family unit. Growing children slowly develop their own ideas and values, becoming opinionated teenagers who question everything, contradict parents, and can be insufferable know-it-alls.

Amongst the first things that go out of the window is the childish belief that mum and dad know best. In fact opposition to parental values is frequently a way of a teenager asserting '*I* know best'. This is often true; parents increasingly know little about what their children are learning in school, and they don't understand the peer group, its culture, its music and its values. They lecture their children about drugs, sex, and rock and roll, but their own understanding is a generation out of date and during that generation that world has moved considerably.

What teenagers see of the world convinces them that the adults haven't done a great job and they think about how things could be better. Young adults become more self-critical and critical of others, often imposing impossibly high standards and expectations. They can be disappointed when they fail to live up to their ideals, or when others let them down. Whilst this is challenging, seeing the old certainties swept away can make young people feel insecure and anxious.

2 Different emotions and how to handle them

Anger (irritability, aggression and rage)

Many teenagers behave badly at home. They are short tempered, often rude and off-hand, and in some cases physically violent. The family is the easiest target for a young person's frustration and anger. Blaming parents can be an easy way out for an adolescent who's having a rough time, and sometimes home is the only place they feel safe enough to express it. Confronting an aggressive, ill-mannered teenager is not easy but there are a few suggestions that parents can try.

■ **Try to minimise damage by taking a step back**

Overreacting, arguing back, shouting or criticising only makes things worse. Try not to get drawn into an argument or shouting match. Calm but firm is more likely to have an effect.

■ **At home, everybody gives vent to emotions that aren't acceptable in the workplace or at social events**

Your teenager probably knows that you will still love and accept them despite their bad temper, but it's not unreasonable for you to expect some self-control at home as well. State your objection

to aggressive behaviour firmly (I don't want you to speak to me like that), in a strong voice with good eye contact. If it continues say what the consequences will be.

■ Outside of the family, most teens will control their temper and be far more easy-going
Try to find out if this is the case – a lack of self-control in the outside world can indicate a more serious problem.

■ If you find your teenager's behaviour unreasonable, discuss it calmly afterwards
Deep down they are probably aware of how badly they are behaving and dislike feeling out of control. Explain the effect they are having on the rest of the family. Be reasonable and non-

confrontational as if expecting their cooperation and you are likely to find they will respond more positively, than if they are lectured or shouted at.

Anger management techniques

Behavioural techniques ('time out'), cognitive techniques such as positive thinking, and experiential techniques like relaxation or guided imagery can all be helpful. Approaches which suit some individuals may not be right for others, so encourage your teenager to try a variety of different methods. Relaxation, taking exercise or getting away from the problem by taking a long walk are good examples.

Angry teenagers are not always noisy and aggressive. Your teen may become quieter and withdrawn, directing their rage inwards. This is less noticeable and often goes undetected by parents. Talking strategies can help. Be aware, however, that internalised anger is harder to spot and, by the time it becomes obvious, has usually been going on for some time.

Confidence (security, self-esteem and pride)

As young people move away from parents for emotional support in favour of their peers, they are withdrawing from the security provided by the family and become subject to all the whims of their contemporaries, including potential rejection. Teenagers react strongly to situations adults find easier to handle, like breaking up with a girlfriend, quarrelling with a friend or failing exams. Adults know from experience that things usually get better but adolescents have never come across these situations before and it hits them hard.

If your teenager is lacking in confidence:

■ Make time for them, give them your undivided attention to talk about the problem

If it's difficult to do that in the house without interruption, try going out together for a walk or for something to eat. The core of any young person's confidence comes from their sense of being loved and supported by their family. It can be easy to

forget this when they appear so confident and independent but make sure they know it.

■ Did something happen that has left your teen feeling rejected and inadequate?

If there are practical things that you can do immediately, do them. For example, if there are academic problems offer your time and assistance. If things don't improve, suggest talking to the teachers together.

Discuss the problem but discourage 'wallowing' – a sympathetic ear is a great help in itself, but avoid reinforcing negative feelings by sympathising too much ('you poor thing'). Be upbeat and positive about what you see as your teen's positive qualities and skills instead ('I know you're finding it hard today but you got excellent grades for your project last week'). Let your child know you think very highly of them and that they are surrounded by family and friends who appreciate them.

■ Let them find their own solution

Teenagers will gain more confidence from sorting out their own problems than from having you do it. Beware of the temptation to take over. There is a limit to what you should do, depending on your son or daughter's age. Younger teens will clearly be more influenced by you and need more help, but different tactics are called for as you move up the age range. It's not always a good idea for you to go wading in to make it right, because you will only increase their sense of helplessness and reinforce the feeling that they are not capable of sorting things out on their own.

■ Listen, don't tell

Ask your teenager to suggest ways in which they believe things can be improved and prompt them to think about the things they are good at. Listen as they find their own solutions and don't rush in with ready-made answers. Once they have sorted their problem, provide practical help if needed. These solutions will be your teenager's own – not yours – and they will be far more likely to act upon them.

Guilt

One of the most significant milestones during early adolescence happens around 10–13 years, when a new capacity for abstract thought starts to develop. This can throw up interesting questions, from the philosophical ('Why does God let wars happen?') to the downright uncomfortable ('You tell me to never lie, but I heard you telling a lie because you didn't want to visit your friend').

Sometimes a little guilt is beneficial and can encourage a teenager not to repeat bad behaviour if they see the hurt it causes. However, some teens suffer from disproportionate guilt over matters which they wrongly perceive to be their 'fault'. Be on the lookout for signs of distress, particularly after traumatic events such as illness or accidents.

Happiness (contentment and elation)

A happy teenager is rarely a problem but mood-swings can show up as extreme exhilaration, over-excitement or arrogance.

Feelings of excessive confidence or invincibility may worry you less, but a teenager who is feeling 'on top of the world' may make rash decisions or take unnecessary risks. Help your teen to recognise the highs as well as the lows and develop techniques for stepping back and taking in situations calmly.

Impatience and impulsiveness

Many parents will complain that their teenagers lack common sense and rush into making decisions without thinking things through. They will often say 'It's their hormones'. But it's not – it's their brains!

In the same way that their bodies are developing, recent research has shown that the teenage brain is still developing too. Connections in the brain, known as synapses, continue forming well into adolescence, and the prefrontal cortex (the area of the brain used to make complex judgements and control impulses) continues changing into the mid-20s. These biological changes in the brain make teenagers more impulsive than adults and more inclined to risk-taking. Other symptoms of a developing brain are overreaction to stressful or uncertain situations and a lack of response to social 'cues'. If you are frustrated by your teenager's lack of thought or tendency to fly off the handle, remember it can be the result of physical causes.

Love and affection

Once they start a relationship, a teen will invest a considerable amount of emotional energy in it and may lose interest in other aspects of life, including family, friends and schoolwork. This can make the break-up of even a short-term relationship very difficult. Youth is no barrier to depth of feeling and some teens are even more passionate in consequence of their lack of experience. Losses can be very painful and healing can take some time.

Many teens settle into longer-term steady relationships, developing strong emotional and sexual bonds with their partners. Many of these relationships will end, which is unsettling and traumatic for both partners, who may become depressed and need considerable support. Accept that they are grieving for the loss of a loved one and don't downplay their feelings – it happens to us all, but there's truth in the old lyric that 'the first cut is the deepest'. Dating different types of people is an important step towards working out what sort of relationship a young adult will want in the longer term. Don't be afraid to seek help if depression becomes extended or severe, or if obsessive or self-destructive behaviour looms.

Showing affection within the family

Now your children are older, it can be more difficult to show affection. Making your teenager feel valued means more than just physical hugs and reassurance. If you are feeling distanced from your teenagers seek out opportunities to spend time and share experiences with them.

- Eat together, either at home or in a restaurant, or buy and share favourite foods.
- Stay in touch – don't just talk to them when there's an 'issue' to discuss, but take an interest in their lives. Now you can enjoy a more adult interaction with them.
- Offer them a lift, if you can. The car is a good place to chat on a journey.
- Watch TV sports or a favourite comedy programme with them.
- Share something of your own life – this will encourage them to tell you about theirs.

Motivation

There are many goals to be achieved during the teenage years, particularly at school. To succeed in public exams requires a considerable amount of persistence and application, and with everything else that is going on during this period in their lives many teenagers find it difficult to keep motivated. If a teenager is lacking in motivation, try to find out the reasons it.

■ Lack of enthusiasm for schoolwork can be down to falling behind in a certain subject or, on the other hand, a failure to be sufficiently stretched in class. It's common for schoolwork to decline in quality at the beginning of secondary school. Your child's head of year can help.
■ Bullying can affect performance at school, but it can also lead to lack of interest in hobbies and sports if the bullying takes place outside of school.
■ Drinking and drug-taking can be behind an apathetic attitude. However, don't jump to conclusions.
■ Some teenagers lose motivation after breaking up with a boyfriend or girlfriend, or falling out with a friend.

Unhappiness – sorrow, grief and depression

Low moods are common during adolescence and nearly all teenagers experience periods of feeling 'down'. In most cases these feelings soon pass, and occasional moodiness or 'bad days' are no cause for alarm. However, it's important to take a young person seriously when they feel depressed. Don't dismiss their unhappiness as excessive or 'just a phase they're going through'.

Teasing or trying to jolly your teen out of it ('You're such a drama queen') is usually counter-productive. Their negative feelings are very real to adolescents – listen, and offer caring, loving support. The concern you offer to friends and colleagues is needed just as much by a young adult at home, and the warning signs that something is seriously wrong are the same.

For more help, contact organisations like mental health charity Young Minds (**www.young minds.org.uk**)

3 When something is seriously wrong

The signs listed below are indicators that something is the matter – it could be drugs, drinking, or an eating disorder, but could just as easily be bullying, school pressures, an unhappy love affair or a physical or mental health problem.

General warning signs

- ☐ Changes in social behaviour – loss of interest in hobbies, sports, and other favourite activities; a new set of friends and/or losing contact with old friends.
- ☐ Changes in the way your teenager acts within the family; deteriorating relationships with family members.
- ☐ Changes in your teenager's academic performance, in school or work attendance and/or a lack of concentration.
- ☐ Physical signs – listlessness, excessive tiredness, lack of appetite, changes in sleeping pattern (eg up at night and sleeping during the day), personal neglect, no interest in grooming.
- ☐ Emotional signs – withdrawal and/or depression, mood-swings, hostile behaviour, lack of co-operation.

Any of these behaviours are common in most teenagers. Warning bells should ring when they are prolonged and show no signs of improvement.

Chapter 4

Friends and social life

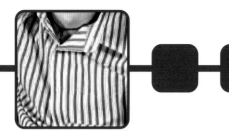

1 Where they go and what they do

With little children, it's simple. Most of their earliest friends were probably relatives', neighbours' or your own friends' children. Now your teenagers' friends are strangers to you, and their values, attitudes, and tastes in music and fashion all come from the peer group. Friends are very important, and asked to choose between family and friends some adolescents will opt for the peer group every time.

When young people embark on a social life of their own making, it's easy to feel excluded and even rejected. You and your home have been the centre of your child's world since they were born, so it is natural to feel a little hurt when they begin to pull away. Try to accept that some distancing is a healthy and normal development as they prepare to enter adulthood. If you can maintain a good relationship with your adolescent, they will talk to you about their friendships and are more likely to bring their friends home. A responsible young person will let you know about their movements, because they know it's the sensible thing to do and they don't want you to worry.

'The young always have the same problem – how to rebel and conform at the same time. They have now solved this by defying their parents and copying one another.'
Quentin Crisp

What's the 'right age'?
In their early teens, both boys and girls want to be allowed out with their friends, first on shopping trips, or trips to the cinema (usually in large groups), or to the home of a friend. As they get towards their mid-teens, they will ask to go out with their friends during the evening. This is where the desire of the child for more freedom clashes with the parents' concerns about safety.

When should teenagers be allowed to go out unsupervised? There are no hard-and-fast rules about the 'right' age. It all depends on:

■ Whether they've got the basic street savvy
Are they able to recognise and avoid danger on the street and are they sufficiently assertive to stand up for themselves. Once they start going to secondary school, most young people learn to travel on public transport and have to deal with street life without the support of their parents. At this point many parents give their children a mobile phone as an extra layer of security, so they can call home if they need help.

■ Their level of maturity
Some 14-year-olds are very responsible and trustworthy – others are not! Age is a good guideline but people develop common sense at different rates.

■ Their physical appearance
Tricky but true. A very young-looking teenager, or one who comes across as nervous, may be vulnerable in situations whereas their friends are fine.

■ Where you live
If you live in a small village you will probably be less worried about allowing them to walk to their friend's house than if they had to travel half-way across London, negotiating the Underground.

■ Who their friends are
If your teenager goes about with a long-established group of mates that you know they can rely on, you're likely to be more lenient than you would be if their gang is made up of new acquaintances who you neither know nor trust. You may also feel happier if their friends are of the same age rather than an older crowd.

■ Where they want to go...
For younger teenagers, local activities like going to the cinema or a friend's house, or to parties with a friend known to the family are one matter, wanting to frequent clubs and bars quite another. If you suspect that there are drugs at these venues, or possibly predatory older people, then say no.

■ ...and how they plan to get home
Make sure that they have safe transport to and from the venue. Decide at what age they are safe to come home on public transport. Arrange with other parents to pick them up when they are first going out. Taxis are expensive, but it's better to pay the fare than have to walk home alone if the last bus has gone. It is better still not to miss that bus in the first place!

2 Friendship

Separating friends from family life is part of a teenager's growing desire for a private life and self-reliance. Avoid criticising your teenager's friends – they seem to resent criticism of their friends, more than criticism of themselves! Be courteous and friendly to their friends – just as you would to a friend of your partner. Be polite rather than pushy, as young people are prone to retreat into monosyllables if they feel they are being probed.

Accept that young people 'try out' friends and partners in the same way that they 'try out' fashions, lifestyles, and even values in their search for a new adult identity. Avoid overreacting and take comfort from the fact that many teenage relationships are transitory!

'Everybody back to mine'

If you can, make your home a welcoming place for friends – though this isn't always easy in a small home. Depending on your resources, a room of their own to hang out in makes a welcome (and safer) alternative to draughty street corners. Noise (and an empty fridge) is a small price to pay for getting to know your teenager's crowd.

Friendship issues

No friends, too few friends, the wrong kind of friends, all of these can become issues for the parents of teenagers. Too many friends may also be worrying if it detracts from schoolwork and academic success.

No friends

Most teens make friends at school. Some teens will hang around in a large group, where others will have one or two friends. Parents need worry only if it seems that their teenager has no friends at all. If your teenager never talks about friends, or if you notice no one phones and they never go out, then there may be a problem. A young person without any friends at school is likely to be depressed and unhappy about it.

Isolated children are susceptible to being bullied, so look out for signs that your child is unhappy or being badly treated at school. Isolation can cause acute unhappiness. Try talking – you can't force your way into a young person's emotional life, but you can be available when they need to talk. Forcing the issue may

lead to clamming up, but the 'active listening' techniques described in Chapter 6 will help.

Ways of opening a conversation might include:

☐ 'Would you like to invite one of your friends to come over this evening?'
☐ 'When you're at school, who do you eat your lunch with?'
☐ 'Is there anyone at school you study with?'

If they have friends but don't go out much, then there is little reason to be concerned. They may spend a lot of time in their room reading, playing computer games or listening to music. It doesn't mean they are insecure or that they don't have friends. It generally occurs in early to mid-teens when they are too young to go out alone but feel increasingly independent of the family. This phase passes when the peer group becomes socially active, and then the problem often becomes one of too much, rather than too little, sociability.

Some pre-teens take time to settle in at secondary school, especially if they haven't moved on with friends from their primary school. By the second year most students will have found themselves one or two close friends or are in with a group. Unpopularity can lower a teen's self-esteem, which makes a difficult situation worse. Go out of your way to give positive reinforcement and build your teen's confidence.

How you can help

There are things parents can do to help their children gain confidence and make friends.

☐ Invite school mates after school, at the weekend or during the holidays.
☐ Find a local drama class or similar social activities that can build confidence.

☐ Encourage teens to join a sports club, especially one with team-based activities.

☐ Encourage them to take on volunteer work, which offers social opportunities and can raise self-esteem.

Money worries

Do they have enough money or the right clothes or gear to join in with groups of kids from school? Check it out with your teen. They may be reluctant to ask, if money is short in the family.

If you get over anxious about the issue, it will increase your teen's stress and make him or her feel more inadequate. Remember that your child's social needs may be different from your own. You may have hung around with a big group when you were a teenager but your teen may be more of a loner, and be happy with fewer friends.

Too many friends

Your son or daughter may have a wide circle of friends and a lively – perhaps too lively – social life. Problems arise when social life takes precedence and schoolwork is neglected.

Don't underestimate the amount of time taken up with homework

The Department for Education and Skills (DfES) guidelines suggest that homework will take between 45mins- 90 minutes each evening in the early years at secondary school to 1.5 hours to 2.5 hours in Year 11. Do the maths! (see Chapter 9 for details). Given the demands of homework, the family meal and some relaxation there is not a lot of time left to go out during the week. Be prepared to give a little on the weekend in return for cooperation during the school week, stressing the importance of getting homework done properly and on time. Staying out late and going to bed late affects a teenager's ability to concentrate at school the next day – not to mention the fact that few parents will want their teenagers hanging around on street corners every evening.

Spell it out

If your teenager is allowed out on a school night, be very clear about your expectations. Don't tell them to 'Come home early', which leaves room for misinterpretation – be deliberate and say 'You need to be home by 10pm'. Clarify the specific time that you expect them to be home. Ask them to ring if they are going to be late so that you won't worry, but don't let them make it a habit. It's considerate to call but it's better to be back on time.

Even when your sociable teenager is at home, friends can be very distracting. As well as telephoning their mates, teens communicate via email and instant messenger programmes such as MSN. If a young person is using the computer for homework a messenger window popping up every few minutes can ruin concentration. Remember that it can be switched off!

Don't like your teenager's friends?

If you don't like your teenager's friends, the first thing to ask yourself is 'Am I being reasonable?' Why do you think they are a bad lot? Are your teenager's friends just different from what you think they should be, in terms of dress, language, diction, music etc, or do you have a more fundamental objection? If you dislike them because of superficial things try not to be judgemental. Obvious disapproval will be viewed as an attack on your teenager's own judgement. Encourage your teenager to invite friends home so you can get the true measure of them.

Are you justified?

Are members of the group egging each other on into dangerous behaviour? Have you heard bad things about them? Do you suspect they are involved with underage drinking, smoking or drug-taking? More seriously, has your teenager's behaviour changed for the worse since joining this group? If you have good reason to believe they are a 'bad crowd' then it is important to try and get your teen away from them. Try to act sooner rather than later, as you will have more influence over a 13-year-old than a 16-year-old.

Getting any teenager to give up their friends is not easy and may not be possible. There are few sanctions parents can impose if their teenager is not prepared to comply. Persuasion is therefore better than force.

- [ ] Get your facts right. If your teen has started slacking off at school or truanting, or if you find evidence of drinking or drug-taking, take a deep breath and talk to your teen about what you know.
- [ ] Calmly state your worries for their health and for their school achievement.
- [ ] Tell them you would like them to stop seeing their friends.
- [ ] If they don't listen, what sanctions can you impose? You can forbid them to go out, and they may or may not comply. You can stop their allowance or pocket money. There are few

effective sanctions, but whatever happens don't give up on talking. If you turn your back on your teenager they will feel even more justified in going their own way.

- [ ] Is there an alternative group they can join? Sports? Drama?
- [ ] A part time job in the evening will get them extra money keep them busy, but make sure there is enough time to do their homework and they don't stay up too late.

This is one of the most difficult problems that the parents of teenagers face. They worry about the danger their child may face from alcohol and drugs and from careless sexual liaisons and fear they will do themselves long-term harm. The majority of teenagers do revert to more normal behaviour as they approach 17 and 18 and many regret the hurt and worry they caused.

> **Don't let your early teen (12–14) just 'hang around' on the street. Try to get him or her involved in extra-curricular activities, which provide opportunities for young people to develop new friendships with, perhaps, different interests. As well as being a great confidence-booster, a commitment to sports and hobbies can demonstrate motivation, sticking-power and initiative to employers and university admissions tutors.**

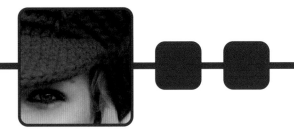

Peer pressure

'But everybody else does....' doesn't have to mean your son or daughter has to do the same.

Peer pressure can be positive

An active group of friends can be a good influence on each other. They can motivate each other to stick to shared sports or other exercise plans. Shared academic aims, such as going to university, can boost a young individual's own aspirations. Peer groups valuing friendship can support teenagers whose home life is not happy and help them through difficult times. Similarly, a mutual dislike of bitching, drug-use or smoking, for example, can encourage positive behaviour within the whole group

Negative peer pressure

Unfortunately the desire to follow the crowd can have unwanted effects, and outsiders are sometimes isolated or bullied. Negative peer pressure can include:

- Competing to have the latest designer clothes or gadgets
- Pressure to smoke, drink too much or experiment with drugs
- Being coerced into unwelcome sexual activity
- Skipping school or making no effort with academic work
- Getting involved in criminal or anti-social activity such as shoplifting or vandalism

The most important thing in resisting peer group pressure is positive family relationships and strong family values. Teens who are loved and respected at home are well prepared to resist negative peer group pressure.

They have self respect and respect for others and someone to turn to for help and advice.

Having good relationships with others in the family means that a teenager feeling under pressure from the peer group has someone to turn to.

Make sure they know the consequences of abusing drugs or booze, sleeping around, failing to get the qualifications they need to get the job they want, or whatever it is that they feel pressured to do. Do they appreciate the long-term results of a criminal record or a sexually transmitted infection (STI)? Provide as much informed advice as you can. Finding out that your teen has been drinking to excess or when underage, dabbling in drugs or is sexually active, can send even the most tolerant parent into a tailspin. This is one of those situations, when your natural impulse to shout, lecture, or threaten should be suppressed. Take a little time to calm down and then sit down with your son or daughter and keeping your cool, have a discussion. You may feel better for letting your emotions out in a tirade but talking calmly is likely to have far more effect. Knowing that you won't get into a state, also means that if you're child has serious issues in these areas they are not afraid to come to you. Encourage your teenagers to seek out information for themselves, at sites such as:

www.talktofrank.com
www.connexions-direct.com

Coming to a conclusion based on their own research and experiences will make it easier for a young person to say 'Sorry, I'm not into that'.

You can help in a practical way by making it easier to walk away. Tell your teenagers that they can call you, or a few designated close family friends, at any time, day or night, and you will come and pick them up, no questions asked and no consequences. Alternatively let them know that there's sufficient money to pay for a taxi in a sealed envelope beside the front door, and there is never any reason to stay in an uncomfortable situation because they feel they can't come home.

See Chapter 8 for more information about drug and alcohol abuse.

Banishing the 'bling'

Pressure to look right and have the 'right' labels is strong in all groups. Even those who are 'anti labels' have their own dress code. It's impossible to fight materialistic peer pressure by upping the amount of pocket money a young person has available, as it's guaranteed to escalate. Parents under pressure to provide their teenagers with the right labels should ask them to think about the following:

■ Is it worth waiting for?

Will they be willing to wait a few months until Christmas or their birthday? Are they happy to put half of their pocket money aside until they have saved enough? If it's not worth the wait, is it worth having?

■ What are they willing to give up?

Can they convert anything they already have into cash? Internet auctions sites, car boot sales and advertisements in free papers now make it easy to sell-on unwanted items. This solution has the bonus of motivating a young person to clean out their room.

■ What happens to the people who don't have the 'must-haves'?

It's upsetting when your son or daughter is teased because they don't have the 'right stuff' but kitting them out in the latest brands is unlikely to resolve the problem. The issue here is bullying, not materialism.

■ Different groups of friends have different values

Is your teenager happy being part of a crowd that judges people according to what they wear or own? How do they feel about making new friends with a less superficial attitude?

■ You don't have to subsidise it

Accept that designer clothes or expensive accessories may be your teenager's top priority. If they really want it, you can't stop them, but you can ensure they earn or save the money to buy it themselves. Say what you would be willing to pay for new trainers and if they can 'top up' the amount with their own money then they can buy them.

■ Don't be emotionally blackmailed

Some parents fear their teenager will resort to shoplifting or other dishonest means if they can't buy or be given what they want. Be absolutely clear that this isn't acceptable.

Bullying

Unpleasant as it is, once identified blatant bullying is a relatively simple issue to tackle. Text or email bullying or physical violence leave concrete evidence that can be used to stop it. More insidious bullying emerges as children get older. Sometimes young people feel the need to cave into peer pressure because they're scared of what might happen if they say no. It's common for bullies to manipulate their victims into being the 'fall guy' – shoplifting on their behalf, for example, or forcing them to be the one who physically harms another victim (despite it having been the bully's idea in the first place).

Bullying doesn't stop at the school gates and many young adults report being bullied in the workplace or on the street. A major problem with bullying is that the victim often doesn't tell. They may feel a sense of shame or be fearful that if they tell, the intimidation will get worse. This means that parents should be on the look out for changes in behaviour that might indicate their teen is being bullied.

Tactics to avoid bullying include:

- Avoiding known situations where bullying occurs, *eg* the local shopping mall, a secluded lane on the way home, or the pub where the bullies hang out.
- Using confident body language to deflect negative attention – stand tall and look people in the eye.
- Walking away from uncomfortable situations and sticking to public places.
- Understanding why bullies feel the need to pick on people – thinking of the bully as an inadequate or jealous person makes it harder to fear them.
- Keeping a diary of any bullying incidents and retaining other proof such as text messages or malicious notes.
- Speaking up – letting friends, family and teachers and/or employers know what's going on. The community police are also happy to help.
- Know your rights. It's mandatory for schools to have anti-bullying policies and employers are legally responsible for preventing bullying and harassing behaviour.

Nobody should have to put up with bullying and everyone has the right to feel safe at school or at work. Help is readily available for anyone concerned about bullying and bringing the problem into the open is the first step towards fixing things.

Useful websites
www.antibullying.net
www.bullying.co.uk
www.bullyonline.org
www.childline.org.uk
www.kidscape.org.uk

The Department for Education and Skills ParentsCentre has information on schools' and local education authorities' obligations towards pupils:

www.parentscentre.gov.uk/ behaviouranddiscipline/bullying

3 Personal safety

Girls are usually portrayed as being more vulnerable than boys, but young men are the people most likely to experience violent street crime. Teenagers of both sexes need to know how to look after themselves. While you can't protect your children against every eventuality, a few commonsense rules will go a long way.

Rules for personal safety

■ **Never hesitate to phone home**
Make sure your teenager understands that you will always be willing to come and get them if they feel uncomfortable or worried – this applies to boys as well as girls.

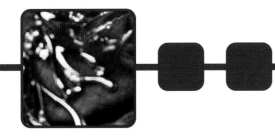

If in doubt, run and shout
The best form of self-defence is to run away and shout for help. Retaliation is potentially very dangerous as the assailant may carry a weapon. A short self-defence course or martial arts class will put the emphasis on avoiding conflict and will build confidence.

Hide your valuables
Flashing around a top-of-the-range mobile phone or carrying a wallet in a back pocket is a temptation to muggers. Obviously expensive white earphones advertise the iPod in their pocket. Spread valuables around your body, *eg* purse in jacket pocket, keys in trouser pocket, so that a mugger won't get everything.

Say where you're going
It's not intrusive, it's basic personal safety, even for adults. Good friends look after each other and it's important that someone knows where they are.

Know where you're going, know how you're getting back
If they're going away from home turf, encourage your teenager to research their route and plan the return journey beforehand. If they need to get a taxi they should remember to take enough money for the fare and find out the number of a registered local minicab firm. Never take an unlicenced minicab hanging around on the street. There's safety in numbers, so stay with the rest of the group whatever the situation and travel back together.

Beware around booze
Drinking too much (or being under the influence of drugs) can make a teenager vulnerable on two counts. Not only are they an easy target for criminals when drunk, they have a false sense of invincibility which leads to taking risks they wouldn't think of taking when sober. If they are worried about drink-spiking, your teenager should buy or mix their own drinks, never leave a drink unattended, and stick to bottled drinks, which are harder to tamper with.

Consider a First Aid course
It's useful for everyone to have a basic grounding in First Aid. Not only can it be a lifesaver in the event of an accident but it will also make your teen more aware of how these accidents can be avoided and reinforce simple safety rules.

Plan ahead
Forewarned is forearmed. Encourage your teenager to plan ahead to avoid problems, or unpleasant incidents. Ask them to 'troubleshoot' before the event – *eg* what would happen in an emergency? How should they protect their SIM card data in case their mobile phone is stolen and they lose all the phone numbers? Would it be sensible to leave an emergency £20 note at home in case they ever need to get a taxi home and don't have enough money? Which neighbours have a spare front door key?

Use the emergency services
Whenever you need to, call 999 without delay. Nobody will get into trouble for calling the police, fire or ambulance service in genuine need.

4 Your teenager's love-life

Coming to terms with a young adult's love-life and sexual identity is one of the most taxing issues to deal with. Common emotions for parents are:

■ Discomfort
Your child is becoming an adult, with adult feelings and sexual needs. This can cause uneasiness as boundaries between parent and child are redrawn.

■ Envy
They are experiencing intoxicating relationships or enjoying a new sense of physical attractiveness in a way that you remember from your own teenage years (or perhaps never had the opportunity to enjoy yourself).

■ Fear
A young person may be emotionally or physically at risk, or you may be concerned by their choice of partner.

■ Jealousy
Your child loves someone other than you and/or has intense emotions that are nothing to do with family life.

■ Rejection
You are not the most important person in their life any more.

Just as children may find the idea of their parents being romantically and sexually involved distasteful, you probably prefer not to dwell on the more personal details of your teenager's love life.

If you don't like their partner
It's sad but true, some of your friends probably have partners you can't stand... but would you tell them about their beloved's shortcomings? Ignoring or criticising your teen's choice will drive a young person away, so try to be non-judgemental. Most teenage relationships are short-lived. Have confidence in your teen's judgement in the long term.

Gay Relationships
If their partner is of the same sex the idea may be more difficult to accept, and parents may also experience more specific concerns, such as whether they will ever have grandchildren, what will relatives of the older generation think, or whether their child will experience discrimination outside the family.

Useful websites
Guidance regarding same sex relationships can be obtained from FFLAG (Families & Friends of Lesbians & Gays, **www.fflag.org.uk**), fpa (formerly the Family Planning Association, **www.fpa.org.uk**), and Brook (**www.brook.org.uk** Freephone 0800 0185023).

If there's a serious problem
See Chapter 8 for guidelines on what to do if you have good reason to be concerned about your teenager's partner's abusive or dangerous behaviour, or are worried about risk-taking when it comes to sex.

> Remember your teenager is still the same person as you have always loved and nurtured, and their sexual identity, although an important part of their character, is only a small portion of what makes up their personality as a whole. They still need love, reassurance and acceptance for who they are.

Chapter 5

Your teenager's health and wellbeing

1 Food and fitness

Eating well

A healthy, balanced diet for a teenager is very similar to that of an adult, although adolescence is a time of rapid growth and it's very important to get enough calories to sustain this. On a daily basis, a teenager should aim to eat:

- ☐ 3–5 servings of vegetables, especially green, leafy vegetables: a serving equals one medium-sized vegetable or equivalent, *eg* eight Brussels sprouts or half a pepper. Potatoes and other related vegetables such as yams and cassava don't count in this category – they are classed as starchy carbohydrate foods.
- ☐ 2–4 servings of fruits: a serving equals one medium-sized fruit or equivalent, *eg* a handful of grapes or one peach.
- ☐ 2–3 servings of protein foods, such as meat, fish, eggs, nuts, or beans: a serving equals one 50–100g portion.
- ☐ 6–11 servings of carbohydrates (grains, rice, bread, cereals, and pasta): a serving equals one slice of bread or 30g of dry cereal.
- ☐ 2–3 servings of dairy products including cheese and yogurt: a serving equals 250ml of milk.
- ☐ At least eight glasses of water or other non-alcoholic, caffeine-free drinks.
- ☐ Occasional consumption of fats, oils, and sweets is fine, just don't overdo it.

The recommended calorie intake for boys aged 9–11 years is about 2,280cal, for 12 to 14-year-olds 2,640cal, and for 15 to 17-year-olds 2,880cal. For girls, it is 2,050cal for 9 to 11-year-olds and 2,150cal for 12 to 17-year-olds.

A few things to bear in mind

■ **The Department of Health recommends that everyone eats at least five portions of fruit and vegetables per day**

This is a minimum guideline, and the more fruit and vegetables in a diet the better. Aim for a variety of colours and flavours to get the most benefit.

■ **Bone density continues to build until the age of 30**

Foods rich in calcium, Vitamin D and phosphorus (dairy, fortified soya products, or canned sardines with bones) help build stronger bones and avoid osteoporosis in later life.

■ **Some teens become anaemic because they don't get enough iron in their diet**

Girls are particularly vulnerable because of their monthly period. As well as red meat, dried fruit (especially figs and apricots), fortified breakfast cereals, green leafy vegetables and even baked beans all contain iron. Having a glass of orange juice (not squash) with a meal is a good idea, as the vitamin C will help the body absorb iron.

■ **There's no reason why a vegetarian diet can't provide everything the body needs**

It's not just a matter of cutting out the meat and fish. Veggies need to plan their menus carefully to avoid missing out on iron, zinc and B-complex vitamins (see The Vegetarian Society's website at **www.vegsoc.org** for more nutritional information). A balanced vegan diet is more challenging but still possible (see **www.vegansociety.com**).

Keeping fit

A high percentage of young people, particularly young girls, are not doing enough exercise. As well as 'formal' exercise like team games or going to the gym, being generally active is important. The recommended 60 minutes of physical activity per day can seem impossible but the little things soon add up.

As well as improving overall fitness, exercise can help confidence and build a better body. The endorphins produced when exercising can make some people feel happier and more peaceful, and regular exercise can also promote sleep. A fit, active body will burn off the empty calories in junk food quickly and with few ill-effects.

There are plenty of opportunities for low-level

exercise to be slotted in during the day, for example:

☐ Cycling or walking to school or college
☐ Taking the stairs rather than the lift
☐ Gardening or household chores
☐ Dancing
☐ Walking briskly around the shops

A 20-minute session of vigorous exercise is also recommended at least three times a week. To get the maximum benefit, experts advise combining different sorts of exercise:

☐ Aerobic exercise which gets the heart pumping faster, and the muscles burning more oxygen. In general, anything that gets you out of breath is aerobic exercise, *eg* basketball, swimming, dancing or just walking quickly.
☐ Strength training to develop the muscles, *eg* rowing, skating or press-ups.
☐ Flexibility training to make the muscles and joints more supple, *eg* gymnastics, ballet or yoga.

Exercising alone can be difficult and boring. Teenagers who prefer individual sports should look for a 'gym buddy' or partner to encourage them to keep going regularly. Joining a team to play sports has the advantage of combining physical exercise with socialising.

2 Self-care and health awareness

Regular check-ups

By the time they are 16, teenagers will probably want to visit the doctor, dentist or optician on their own. This is a normal sign of growing independence. Make sure your adolescent is aware of the importance of regular health checks, how often they should happen, and what is available to them.

At the time of writing free NHS eye tests are available to anyone under 16, or under 19 and in full-time education. Opticians recommend an eye test every two years and it's particularly important to have your eyesight assessed before learning to drive.

NHS dental treatment is free for people aged under 18 (or aged 18 but in full-time education). Until recently a dental check-up every six months was recommended. However, new guidelines suggest the patient and dentist arrange their own timetable depending on individual needs, which can be more frequent than the tradition bi-annual check.

Although cervical smear tests are free on the NHS for women aged 25–49 it is recommended that testing begins three years after an individual first becomes sexually active. Smear tests are carried out every three years, unless there is a medical reason for more frequent testing.

Self-examination

Breast examination and testicular examination are important. Although most will turn out to be harmless, any lumps should be immediately seen by a doctor.

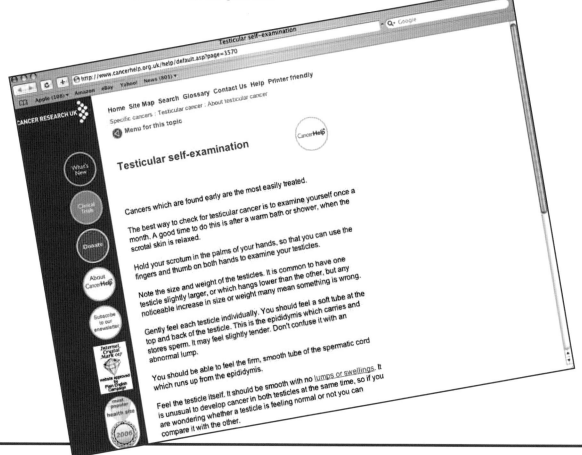

3 Immunisation

BCG (Bacillus Calmette-Guerin)
The BCG jab against tuberculosis is now just a memory. Since September 2005, 14-year-olds are no longer offered the injection as a matter of course. A new, targeted programme means that only those at high risk of TB (including babies and older people) will now be vaccinated.

Influenza (flu)
It's recommended that vulnerable groups, such as the elderly or people with a weakened immune system, get a flu jab every autumn, between late September and early November. The flu jab is not considered a necessity for fit, healthy teenagers but they may wish to consider it if a dose of flu would cause severe problems, *eg* if they have exams or are in their first term at university. It's likely that they (or you) will have to pay for the injection unless they are in a vulnerable category.

Meningitis
It is now possible to be immunised against both Meningococcal C and Hib Meningitis but the vaccine is not given routinely. Health experts will advise when immunisation is necessary, usually when there has been an outbreak in a school or on campus. Unfortunately, these injections do not protect against all forms of the disease (there is still no vaccine to protect against the most common form of infection, which is the 'B' strain). See Chapter 5 for warning signs of meningitis.

Td/IPV (Diphtheria, Tetanus and Polio)
Teenagers will probably have had most of their inoculations before they started school. However, between the ages of 13 and 18 they will be offered the combined Td/IPV vaccination. This is a single jab (given in the upper arm) that protects against all three diseases.

Tetanus
If your teenager has received all their scheduled childhood vaccinations they will only need a tetanus booster if they are at risk of getting tetanus following an injury in the future. The Td/IPV inoculation gives immunity for ten years, so there's nothing to worry about until they're 23 at least!

Useful website
www.immunisation.org.uk

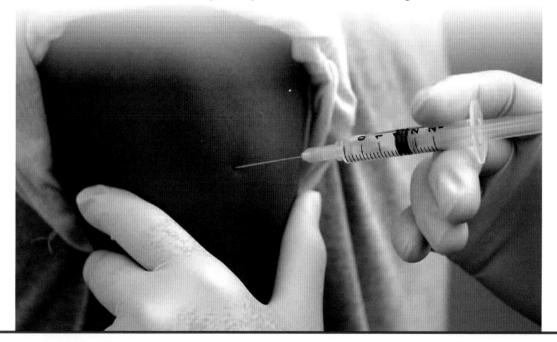

4 Holiday health

If your teenager is planning an exotic holiday or Gap Year in a far-flung region, it's important that they are protected against serious diseases.

Travel jabs

GPs will be able to advise about which jabs are needed. Make an appointment at least eight weeks before the departure date, as some vaccines have to be administered well in advance. Free travel vaccinations vary across practices, but usually include Typhoid, Hepatitis A, and Meningitis C. There is normally a charge for Yellow Fever, Rabies, Japanese Encephalitis, Hepatitis B jabs and others.

Malaria

Around 1,750 travellers return to the UK with malaria each year – don't let your teenager become one of them. No anti-malaria pill is 100 per cent effective so it makes sense to use insect repellent and mosquito nets when staying in a malarial region.

IMPORTANT: Anti-malarial drugs need to be taken before, during and after the trip, exactly as and when prescribed, taking care not to miss any doses.

Safe and sensible behaviour

There is a tendency for teens (and older people) to take more risks on holiday than they would if they were at home. Remind them that accepting lifts from strangers, swimming in a strong current, driving without a seatbelt etc is as reckless abroad as in the UK.

Useful website
www.fitfortravel.nhs.uk

5 Common complaints

Teenagers are only human – difficult as this may be to believe, sometimes – and get pretty much the same illnesses as the rest of us. It would be impossible to cover all of the health issues here, so we've concentrated on the most common complaints encountered during adolescence.

Please remember that no book can ever be a substitute for professional medical advice. Your doctor knows best. In an emergency, don't hesitate to call 999.

Acne

It's a rare teenager who makes it through to adulthood without experiencing the odd zit. Severe acne, however, can make a teen's life a misery and, in extreme cases, can lead to bullying, shyness or depression. At a time when most adolescents are self-conscious, even mild acne can feel very serious.

Causes

There's no scientific evidence pointing to chocolate, chips, or even stress as the cause. Acne is due to overactive sebaceous glands making too much sebum, the oil that lubricates hair and skin. The sebaceous glands can become over-stimulated by the hormones produced during puberty. An unhealthy diet and stressful lifestyle can make acne worse but will not bring it on in the first place. Acne is not 'dirty'; on the contrary, washing the face too much can dry it out and make the sebaceous glands work even harder to compensate.

Signs and symptoms

Acne usually appears on the face but can also occur on the back, shoulders, neck, chest, and on other parts of the body such as the groin. Greasy skin and clogged pores lead to blackheads and whiteheads, which start off about the size of a pencil point but can grow up to the size of the blunt end of a pen. If bacteria, sebum and dead skin cells invade the blocked pore, this results in spots and pimples, sometimes with a pus-filled top as the body fights the bacterial infection. The build-up of matter in a clogged pore can end up as a large, painful lump deep in the skin. These lumps – known as nodules or cysts – can leave permanent scars.

Prevention and treatment

To some extent, spots are inevitable. However, a good diet rich in zinc and vitamins A and C will help your teenager to achieve clearer skin. Vitamin E has been proven to lessen the severity of scarring and is beneficial for the skin in general – there should be no need to take pills and supplements if your teen has a balanced diet. Drinking about eight glasses of water every day flushes out impurities and keeps the skin hydrated.

Don't pick at it! Squeezing can spread bacterial infection and cause long-term scarring. Expensive cosmetics and non-prescription facial treatments can irritate the skin and do more harm than good. If acne is a problem for your teenager, especially if it is affecting their confidence, your GP will be able to help. Creams, antibiotics or hormonal treatments (the contraceptive pill) are the first resort, to be followed by stronger medications or even laser therapy if unsuccessful. Acne tends to peak at 17–18 in girls and 19–20 in boys, so reassure your teenager it shouldn't last for ever.

Athlete's Foot

Athlete's Foot is caused by a fungus that thrives in warm, dark, humid conditions... a teenager's musty trainer is the perfect environment!

Causes

Athlete's Foot often emerges in the teenage years, sometimes because of slapdash hygiene but also because changing rooms and swimming pools frequented by teens are the ideal breeding ground for the fungus.

Signs and symptoms

Dry, itchy skin between the toes is usually the first sign of Athlete's Foot. If left untreated it can lead to scaling, inflammation and painful blisters and spread to the nail, where it is difficult to eradicate.

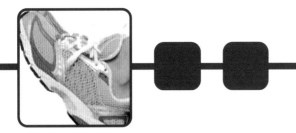

Prevention and treatment

Careful attention to hygiene is important. Make sure teens dry their feet thoroughly, especially between the toes, and change their socks regularly (natural fibre socks are best, as these help the feet breathe). If Athlete's Foot is present, then don't use the same towel again until it has been thoroughly laundered. Drying the feet with a hair dryer ensures that they are totally dry and that there is no cross contamination to towels. Teens should avoid wearing the same pair of shoes all the time and should never share shoes. Antifungal foot powder can be bought over the counter from your pharmacist. If the infection fails to respond, your doctor can provide antifungal medication plus antibiotics to treat any secondary infection.

Braces

Once adult teeth appear your dentist may recommend orthodontic treatment. This can be for cosmetic reasons (to straighten the teeth) or to prevent problems in later life caused by poor alignment of the teeth, gums and jaw joints and irregular biting pressure.

Braces can be uncomfortable at first. Unaccustomed pressure can lead to pain in the jaw or teeth, and/or headaches, which can interfere with sleeping and eating for a few days. Over-the-counter painkillers can be helpful but, if the discomfort continues for more than a few days, or if pressure from the appliance causes sore spots or ulcers inside of the mouth, go back and seek your dentist's advice.

Both teeth and braces need to be cleaned very thoroughly, otherwise pieces of food will get trapped. If your teenager develops bad breath after having braces fitted they may need to pay more attention to oral hygiene. Flossing and using toothpicks, miniature dental brushes and a mouthwash can oust the particles that a toothbrush can't reach.

Bruises, sprains, and strains

Teenagers tend to be accident-prone, particularly during growth spurts. They are also keen to try out their new physical strength at sports and hobbies, and sometimes underestimate their limitations.

Signs and symptoms

A bruise is a discoloured area on the skin, caused by a blow that breaks the blood vessels under the

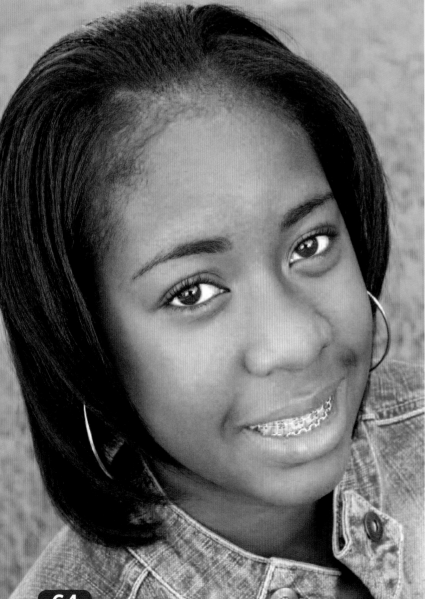

skin. Although bruises can look dramatic they are rarely dangerous. A sprain is caused by the same principle but centres around a joint and is usually more painful and swollen.

If the injury is very painful, if your teenager heard a 'pop' when the accident took place, if there is any loss of mobility, or if things don't improve after 48 hours, seek medical advice – they may have torn a ligament or broken a bone.

Blows to the head should always be taken seriously. See the First Aid check list in Section 7 for the signs of concussion.

Prevention and treatment

If your adolescent enjoys sports, exercise or dance classes, check they are supervised by a qualified instructor who will emphasise the need to warm up and stretch beforehand.

Most bruises do not require treatment but a cold pack applied early on can help reduce the discolouration and pain. Simple sprains and strains can be treated at home using rest, ice, compression and elevation (RICE):

☐ Rest the injured limb for the first 24 to 48 hours to prevent any further injury.

☐ Ice will cool the damaged area and is effective for up to 24 hours after the injury. Use a cold-pack or a packet of frozen peas wrapped in a tea towel, but don't put it in direct contact with the skin or the patient could get frostbite. Use the cold-pack for up to 20 minutes every hour, but for no longer than three hours in all.

☐ Compression must be firm but not too tight (blood still needs to circulate). Elasticated bandages are effective.

☐ Elevate the affected area above heart level if possible. Ideally, persuade your teenager to lie down and elevate the limb with a few pillows, or use a chair or table. Elevation should be maintained for a few days.

An Ibuprofen-based painkiller will help reduce swelling and discomfort.

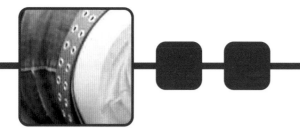

The odd knock probably won't do any long-term harm and may actually be a timely reminder to your teen that they are not indestructible. However, repeated and unexplained bumps and bruises could be a sign your child is being bullied, or is taking risks after drinking. If you are worried, see sections 6 and 8 for advice on talking to teens and working through difficult issues.

Cold sores

Cold sores can be a source of anguish to teens, as, being around the mouth area, they are very noticeable and unsightly.

Causes

A cold sore is caused by the herpes simplex virus, via skin-to-skin contact. The virus can lie dormant, and although some people only ever have one attack they can recur throughout life.

Signs and symptoms

A cold sore is an itchy, fluid-filled blister on a raised, red, painful area on the lips or around the mouth. Attacks are often heralded by tingling in the affected area and a small hard spot that can't yet be seen. They usually last 7–10 days.

Prevention and treatment

Though you can't cure or prevent cold sores, you can take steps to reduce their frequency and to limit the duration of an occurrence. Cold sores often flare up when the immune system is low or a person is stressed. Cold sores are picked up from another person who has an active lesion.

Shared eating utensils, razors and towels may spread the infection, A healthy, balanced diet and enough sleep can sometimes hold them at bay. Bright sunlight can also bring them on, so a lip balm containing sunblock will help. If an attack is on its way some people find that holding an ice-cube on the affected area before the sore is visible prevents it from developing. There are several effective topical creams that can be applied in the early stages to stop the sore from developing. Ask your pharmacist to recommend one.

Remember your teen may be embarrassed and upset by a cold sore, and may even want to take a day off school until it is less obvious.

Glandular Fever (infectious mononucleosis)

Sometimes known as the 'kissing disease', glandular fever is more often spread by airborne droplets. It is common amongst teenagers and easily spread between groups of people at schools and colleges.

Causes
The Epstein-Barr virus which causes Glandular Fever has an incubation period of 30–50 days. It is easily spread, as most people don't realise they are infected until they have had a month to spread it around!

Signs and symptoms
Flu-like symptoms may precede Glandular Fever. The main symptoms are swollen lymph nodes in the throat, armpits and groin, and extreme fatigue with muscle pains, headaches, fever and a tendency to sweat. Other symptoms include a sore throat, swollen tonsils with a whitish coating, stomach pains and rash. In some cases there may be signs of enlarged spleen and liver, and jaundice. A blood test and throat swab by your doctor will confirm diagnosis.

Prevention and treatment
Rest is essential. Avoid exercise at first. Expect your teenager to take at least four weeks to get back to normal physical activity. Don't allow them to push themselves if they get tired – they need to take it easy or recovery will be longer. Plenty of fluids and small, light meals can help but, unfortunately, there is no effective treatment for Glandular Fever other than time. It is important to avoid alcohol

for six weeks after contracting the infection, to avoid putting extra strain on the liver.

It can take a patient months to fully recover form the virus, but once a person has had Glandular Fever they develop a lifelong immunity to it.

Growing pains
During growth spurts, otherwise healthy adolescents may complain of pains in the limbs, particularly at night.

Causes
Little is known about the causes of growing pains, and the name itself may be a misnomer. Some doctors believe they are caused by muscle strain from physical activity during the day.

Signs and symptoms
Throbbing pains in the legs, without any obvious cause or injury, which respond well to massage and heat. Most people with growing pains do not experience them every day and usually only suffer from them at night.

Prevention and treatment
Non-prescription painkillers (such as paracetamol) can help, as can a hot-water bottle applied to the painful area. A muscle-stretching programme, developed in Canada in the 1980s, has shown good results in combating growing pains. Stretching the calf and thigh muscles of each leg twice before bedtime, for around 20–30 seconds each time, can relieve the discomfort.

Irritable Bowel Syndrome (IBS)
IBS is an increasingly common teenage complaint, for reasons yet unknown. It's possible that the dietary changes and more irregular eating habits that occur when teenagers start taking more responsibility for feeding themselves can cause a flare-up. In girls, the hormonal fluctuations of the menstrual cycle can be related to IBS.

Causes
The causes of IBS are not fully understood but it

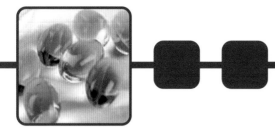

has been suggested that food intolerance and stress may play a part.

Signs and symptoms

Wind, constipation, diarrhoea, bloating, or a combination of these symptoms with no obvious other cause. All these symptoms may be caused by other conditions, which your doctor can test for and eliminate.

Prevention and treatment

A healthy diet with plenty of roughage can help, as can exercise. Eating at regular times of the day can keep the bowel functioning smoothly. Avoid faddy dieting. If stress is a trigger, relaxation techniques can be of benefit.

Useful website
www.ibsnetwork.org.uk

Panic Attacks

Panic attacks can be deeply distressing but, in themselves, cause no long-term harm.

Causes

Anxiety, phobia, stress and/or depression can trigger panic attacks.

Signs and symptoms

Symptoms can include feeling dizzy or faint, palpitations, sweating, trembling or shaking, difficulty breathing, chest pain, fear of dying or a sensation of dread. A panic attack can be very frightening.

Prevention and treatment

The long-term solution is to address the underlying problems causing the attacks. Your GP may recommend that severe and frequent panic attacks are treated by cognitive behaviour therapy (CBT) or drugs. However, in the short-term techniques such as controlled breathing into a paper bag or cupped hands can calm a teenager experiencing a panic attack.

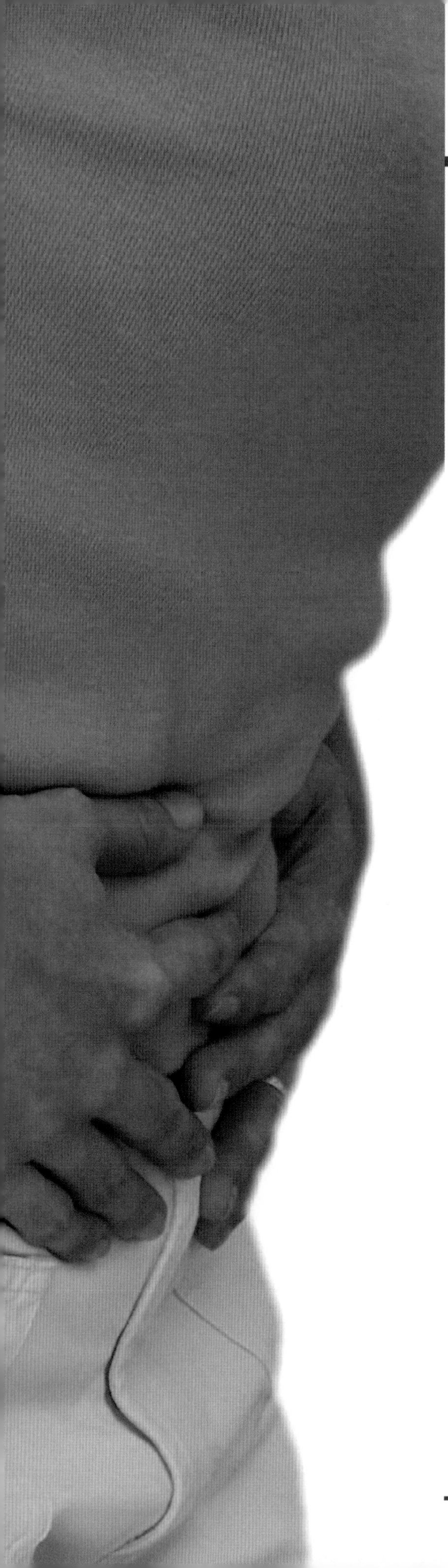

Period Pain (dysmenorrhoea)

The level of discomfort varies greatly. Some teenagers have very little trouble, whereas for others the pain can severely disrupt their lives.

Causes

The hormones that cause the muscles of the uterus to contract and help expel the menstrual blood can also cause painful cramps and other unpleasant symptoms.

Signs and symptoms

Some girls experience pain during the first years of menstruation or begin to experience pre-menstrual bloating and heavy or irregular bleeding. Sometimes the cramps are severe, and may be accompanied by feeling faint, headaches, diarrhoea, nausea and vomiting. Pain can extend to the thighs and lower back and is usually most severe during the first few days of menstruation.

Prevention and treatment

Over-the-counter painkillers such as codeine and ibuprofen are readily available, and the pharmacist may recommend specially formulated painkillers for menstruating girls. Taking painkillers just before the onset of the period, if your daughter can predict it, can lessen the severity. Sometimes a hot-water bottle applied to the lower stomach can be soothing.

Some girls need to spend a few hours lying down when cramps are at their worst. Girls at school may need to leave the classroom.

Your doctor can help with severe symptoms. It's an important time for your daughter, both academically and socially, so don't be fobbed off with 'it's just her age'.

A number of complementary treatments, such as calcium and magnesium supplements, are often recommended for painful periods, as is Angus Castus and evening primrose oil. Some nutritionists advise eating starchy food, little and often. However, as with any treatment there's no substitute for the advice of a qualified

professional.

Repetitive Strain Injury (RSI)

As teenagers spend more and more time at a computer keyboard RSI is becoming a common problem.

Causes

Repeated small movements – *eg* using a computer mouse or games console – can result in RSI, especially when they are carried out over long periods without a break. Practising for hours on musical instruments can also cause RSI.

Signs and symptoms

RSI often begins with a slight ache in one or both hands or wrists. If this is ignored it can lead to pain and tingling in the joints, shoulders, neck and back.

Prevention and treatment

Specialists recommend spending no longer than 20 minutes at a keyboard without a short break, so encourage your teenager to take time off to stretch and relax. Remind them that most computer games have 'pause' buttons! A proper seat and well-positioned screen and keyboard are essential when working at a computer.

In severe cases, over-the-counter painkillers or hot packs can help. However, if the RSI is this bad it's vital for your teen to take a few days away from the computer and games console to allow their body to recover, or permanent injury could result.

6 Warning signs

Alcohol poisoning and dependence

Despite the worry and publicity around illegal drugs, teenagers are more likely to have problems relating to alcohol: it's easy to get hold of and socially acceptable. The biggest dangers to a teenager are risky behaviour when drunk, and excessive consumption of alcohol that leads to vomiting and unconsciousness.

If you find your teenager has drunk too much, it's possible that all they may need is a good night's rest and an aspirin in the morning. However, young teens whose bodies are not fully developed may develop alcohol poisoning, which is far more dangerous and can even be fatal. Be on the alert for the following symptoms and teach your teenagers to do the same, if their friends are drinking to excess. In cases of alcohol poisoning, leaving someone to 'sleep it off' can kill.

A person suffering from alcohol poisoning may:

- ☐ Vomit
- ☐ Lose control of their bladder and/or bowels
- ☐ Pass out and/or lapse in and out of consciousness, becoming difficult to rouse
- ☐ Have slow, noisy breathing and dilated pupils
- ☐ Their skin may be cold and clammy to the touch

If you think a teenager has been drinking and they display any of these symptoms, call an ambulance. While you are waiting for it to arrive, make sure they are lying on their side so that their airway will be clear if they vomit. Don't leave them alone. A trip to casualty following a drinking binge is a deeply unpleasant experience but it's better to be safe than sorry.

Alcohol dependence is less common in teenagers. However, a teen who shows any of the following behaviour may be at risk of developing a long-term problem:

- ☐ Relies on drink to get them through social events
- ☐ Finds it difficult to go without a drink
- ☐ Worries that alcohol is affecting schoolwork
- ☐ Spends large sums of money on drink
- ☐ Indulges in regular binge drinking

Useful websites

Organisations such as **www.alcoholconcern.org.uk** and **www.talktofrank.com** can offer information and advice. Al-Anon (**www.al-anonuk.org.uk**) offers support to the families of people who have a problem with alcohol and drugs, while **www.thesite.org/drinkanddrugs** is specifically aimed at teenagers.

Drugs

Try to avoid thinking in terms of 'signs and symptoms' of drug abuse. Trying to spot 'warning signs' is no substitute for good communication.

Look out for changes in social and family interaction and performance at school. Checklists

can be useful within reason but there is always a danger of jumping to the wrong conclusion, or creating an atmosphere of mistrust within the family. If you're concerned that there's something wrong with your teenager, or that they are acting strangely, talking is far better than looking for pointers to specific problems.

We have already described general signs of a possible problem in Chapter 3, but drug-specific physical signs can include listlessness, excessive tiredness, lack of appetite, and red-rimmed eyes and/or runny nose (without allergies or a cold).

If you think you have good reason to suspect drug use, also look out for paraphernalia such as pipes, rolling papers, small medicine bottles, eye drops, butane lighters, homemade pipes or bongs (pipes that use water as a filter) made from soft drinks cans or plastic beverage containers, scorched tinfoil, razor blades and syringes.

Useful websites
Useful websites for parents and teenagers worried about drugs include **www.talktofrank.com** and **www.connexions-direct.com**.

Eating disorders (anorexia and bulimia)
Adolescent girls and young women are perceived as being vulnerable to eating disorders but they are becoming increasingly common amongst males and pre-pubescent children too.

Anorexia nervosa
Anorexia is an eating disorder that usually begins around the onset of puberty. Individuals suffering from anorexia undergo extreme weight loss as they gradually starve themselves. Weight loss is usually 15 per cent below the person's normal body weight. As well as not eating the young person may also exercise excessively and use laxatives.

People with anorexia continue to think they are overweight even after they become extremely thin, are very ill or are near death. Often they will develop strange eating habits, such as refusing to eat in front of other people. Sometimes anorexics will prepare big meals for others while refusing to eat any of it themselves.

Early warning signs include changes in eating habits such as:

☐ Cutting out whole food stuffs like fats or carbohydrates.

☐ Claiming not to be hungry or to have already eaten.
☐ Refusing to eat by claiming to feel sick or unwell.
☐ Consuming bulky but low-calorie foods such as lettuce or cucumber.
☐ Pushing food around the plate without eating anything.
☐ Removing food from the plate and hiding it to dispose of later.
☐ Excessive exercising.

It is not unusual for healthy teens to start watching what they eat. Taking up exercise is something to be encouraged. What marks out anorexics is the degree to which they do these things. This means that it may be quite some time before parents become aware of what is happening.

Anorexics will become rapidly and painfully thin but will often wear layers of loose clothes to disguise it. Beware of bouts of constipation or diarrhoea (which can hint at abuse of laxatives). If anorexia becomes extreme, a girl's periods will stop and downy hair may start growing on her face. In both sexes, nails and hair will become brittle.

Bulimia nervosa
Bulimia sufferers usually maintain a 'normal' body weight, but will eat and then vomit up abnormal amounts of food. Large quantities of 'junk food' – ie fatty, sweet or starchy foods – are usually consumed within a short time. Indications of bulimic behaviour include:

☐ Packets of biscuits, ice cream, tinned food, jam, bread, bottles of cooking oil or whole jars of peanut butter suddenly disappearing.
☐ Food may be hoarded or hidden in cupboards.
☐ Bins full of wrappers from chocolate, biscuits and other foodstuffs.
☐ Dehydration and constipation caused by constant vomiting, which deprives the sufferer of proteins, carbohydrates and potassium.

☐ Dry skin and/or a puffy face.
☐ The bathroom constantly smells of air-freshening spray, used to mask the smell of vomit.
☐ The enamel of the teeth deteriorating due to stomach acids being regurgitated.

What to do about eating disorders
If you are concerned that your teen is suffering from either anorexia or bulimia, provide support and encouragement without intruding and seek professional help as soon as you can. Argument and persuasion from family members is seldom productive.

To the majority of teens with eating disorders, it appears that their body-weight is the only area of their life over which they have control. They may therefore be very resistant to getting treatment, which they feel will take away that control. It is vital to approach the problem with tact. Remember, boys are at risk as well as girls.

Sufferers need professional help – the earlier, the better. Ask your GP to recommend a specialist clinic.

Meningitis
Meningitis is a dangerous disease with a swift onset. If you suspect your teenager has meningitis, you should consult a doctor immediately. The initial symptoms can resemble flu. Look out for:

☐ Confusion, sleepiness and/or loss of consciousness
☐ Difficulty walking or standing
☐ Dislike of bright lights
☐ Fever
☐ Headache
☐ Pain in the limbs or stomach
☐ Shivering and/or icy-cold hands and feet
☐ Stiff neck
☐ Vomiting

Sometimes, but not always, a blotchy red and purple rash accompanies the onset of meningitis.

If a tumbler is rolled firmly over the rash and it doesn't disappear with the pressure of the glass, then get medical attention without delay. This could be a symptom of septicaemia.

Mental health

Depression
Parents are often uncertain whether their teen is really depressed or simply 'low'. Depression is not simply normal sadness but a serious illness that causes both physical and psychological symptoms. Depression is common during adolescence but is often not recognised or treated.

Common behaviours associated with depression include:

- ☐ Being awake throughout the night
- ☐ Being reckless or taking unnecessary risks (*eg* driving fast or dangerously)
- ☐ Drug abuse, truancy, violence or petty theft
- ☐ Increased alcohol and drug use
- ☐ Increased irritability and frustration
- ☐ Increased physical health complaints like fatigue or pain
- ☐ Loss of interest in food, sex, exercise or other pleasurable activities
- ☐ Moodiness that is out of proportion to recent events
- ☐ More sensitivity to minor personal criticisms
- ☐ Staying home from work or school
- ☐ Weepiness
- ☐ Withdrawal from social events

Many of these behaviours are common in adolescence. What marks out depression in young people is the extent of these behaviours, and the length of time they persist.

Anxiety
Anxiety is a normal reaction to stress. A little anxiety helps teens to focus on studying for an exam or an important social event. But when anxiety becomes an excessive, irrational dread of

everyday situations it becomes a disabling disorder.

If you notice any behavioural changes that last for a period of two weeks or more in close family or friends, it is possible that the person has an unrecognised anxiety disorder. Common behaviours associated with anxiety include:

- ☐ Avoiding crowded places like the cinema, shopping centre, or public transport.
- ☐ Increased irritability and sensitivity to criticism.
- ☐ Increased use of alcohol and drugs, particularly in social situations.
- ☐ Increased worrying about common problems like finance, work or family relationships.
- ☐ Not being able to go to sleep.
- ☐ Panic attacks.
- ☐ Unable to finish school or work projects.
- ☐ Unwilling to go out and socialise.

Bi-polar disorder
The first signs of bi-polar disorder (formerly known as manic-depression) often manifest during adolescence. The most obvious symptoms are extreme mood swings, beyond the norm for adolescents. These range from extreme happiness and elation (mania) to extreme sadness and withdrawal (depression). Episodes can last several weeks or more. Some people experience 'rapid cycling', when they swing from high to low without having a 'normal' period in between.

Bi-polar episodes are very pronounced and different from mainstream mood-swings. It's important to contact your GP, regardless of your child's potential resistance to your intervention.

Schizophrenia
Schizophrenics usually start behaving in an 'abnormal' way because they are responding to their changed perception of the world. It often begins during early adulthood and can make a young person very vulnerable.

Schizophrenics are prone to delusions (abnormal beliefs not based in reality) and hallucinations (the sensation of an experience that isn't actually happening). They can follow up their delusions and hallucinations with thoughts and actions which make perfect sense to them but, being based on abnormal beliefs, are inappropriate for day-to-day life.

In such situations you must seek medical help without delay.

Helping somebody with a mental health problem
Someone who is going through mental health problems is not easy to live with. One of the consequences of their problem is that other family members may withdraw and stop trying to help. Parents should seek professional help, even though their teen may resist treatment. Some disorders require medical intervention.

Useful website
www.youngminds.org.uk is a website for adolescents that answers some of their questions about depression and anxiety.

Self-harm
Causing superficial injuries, such as cuts or burns, is a way of expressing deeper pain. Teenagers who do this to themselves may go to great lengths to conceal their injuries. Look out for:

- ☐ The wearing of long-sleeved clothing in hot weather.
- ☐ Avoidance of situations, such as swimming pools, in which the required clothing might expose wounds.
- ☐ Unusual scars or injuries that lack a reasonable explanation – self-harmers' injuries often form regular patterns or shapes (such as an 'X' or a circle of cigarette burns) which are unlikely to be caused by an accident.
- ☐ Sharp objects such as razor blades or needles going missing around the home, and First Aid supplies – *eg* antiseptic and sticking plasters – needing to be replaced more often than normal.
- ☐ Blood-stained tissues or clothing.

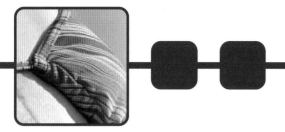

Sex – risky behaviour

Although safe sex is heavily promoted in schools and the media, a growing number of young people seem to be ignoring the message, and the incidence of sexually transmitted infections is growing in the UK. Despite recent medical advances HIV remains incurable and ultimately fatal. Other diseases such as chlamydia, gonorrhoea and syphilis can lead to permanent infertility. Herpes, pubic lice and viral warts are other undesirable conditions that can result from unprotected sexual contact.

Prevention is better than cure. Make sure your teenager knows and abides by basic safe sex rules, which can also guard against unwanted pregnancies:

- ☐ Use a condom, or other barrier method, during sex.
- ☐ Sex is not all about penetration and there are many ways to enjoy sexual contact without health risks.
- ☐ Avoid casual sex or careless unprotected sex when drunk or high.
- ☐ Say 'no' to any sexual act that you are uncomfortable with.
- ☐ Don't rely on the promises of a potential partner, protect yourself. If in doubt, use a condom.

7 First Aid

Do you know what to do in an emergency? Even if you do, your teenager won't always be with you. As a parent you probably already know the basics of First Aid. For a young person it's a vital skill that could save their own life or that of others.

What follows is only a brief outline. There's no substitute for proper training by experts. St John Ambulance run courses that are open to anyone over 10 (see **www.sja.org.uk** for details).

NB These guidelines only cover procedures for teenagers and adults. In some instances, such as CPR (cardio-pulmonary resuscitation), the procedure varies with age.

A few basic rules

☐ Do only what's immediately essential and dial 999.

☐ Avoid leaving a casualty unattended.

☐ If you don't know what to do, don't do it – doing the wrong thing can be more harmful than the accident itself.

☐ Act quickly when you have to: start CPR immediately, plunge burns into water without delay, and apply pressure to stop serious bleeding at once.

☐ Don't move a victim unless it's essential to prevent further harm.

☐ Place anyone who is unconscious in the recovery position, on their side (see right).

☐ Give nothing to eat or drink, as this can delay treatment.

☐ Cover an injured person lightly to keep them warm and provide lots of reassurance, even if you think they can't hear you.

☐ For less serious injuries, call the NHS Direct 24-hour Helpline on 0845 4647.

If you're the first person at the scene of an accident

Check for a response – is the casualty conscious? If not, assess them using ABC:

☐ **Airway** Can they breathe freely or is the airway blocked?

☐ **Breathing** Can the casualty breathe independently?

☐ **Circulation** Can you feel their pulse? Does the casualty's colour and/or ability to move indicate good circulation?

Recovery position

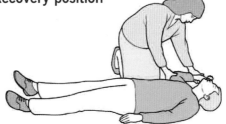

If breathing has stopped, or the person is not breathing normally

DIAL 999 FOR AN AMBULANCE then start cardio-pulmonary resuscitation (CPR), which is a combination of chest compressions and 'rescue breaths':

- [ ] Place your hands on the centre of the casualty's chest and, with the heel of your hand, press down 4–5cm.
- [ ] After every 30 such chest compressions give two breaths: pinch the person's nose, place your mouth over their mouth and – by blowing steadily – attempt two rescue breaths, each lasting more than one second.
- [ ] Continue with cycles of 30 chest compressions and two rescue breaths until emergency help arrives or the person begins to breathe normally.

If the casualty is unconscious

- [ ] Unconsciousness may follow a head injury or stroke. Diabetics can lapse into a coma if blood sugar levels fall or rise out of control.
- [ ] Unconsciousness is a serious symptom. Call an ambulance and be prepared to administer CPR if the casualty's condition deteriorates.
- [ ] Place the casualty in the recovery position to minimise the danger of choking.
- [ ] A person can suffer concussion without loss of consciousness. If they are dizzy/nauseous, pale, confused, or are suffering from loss of memory after a head injury, call a doctor unless the casualty returns to normal very quickly.
- [ ] Convulsions can be a sign of brain injury and are upsetting to watch. Unless you're certain someone is a known epileptic, don't hesitate to get medical help.
- [ ] If an epileptic fit occurs, try to break the person's fall if you can and clear any dangerous objects out of the way. Loosen clothing and try to put something soft under or around their head to protect it. Do not restrain the person. The fit should pass relatively quickly.

Severe bleeding

- [ ] Call for help. Lay the casualty flat and if possible raise the source of the bleeding above the height of the heart.
- [ ] Act fast to apply pressure, using a clean towel, scarf, handkerchief etc or your hand. Squeeze the edges of a bleeding cut together.
- [ ] If a pad becomes saturated, don't take it off. Apply another on top of it.
- [ ] DON'T apply a tourniquet – this can be dangerous or even fatal.

Burns and scalds

- [ ] Leave the burn alone as far as possible. Don't try to remove burnt clothing etc but take off jewellery, as swelling might make rings or bracelets irremovable.
- [ ] Submerge the burn in cold water immediately and keep it submerged until trained medical help arrives.

Suspected internal injuries or fractures

- [ ] Don't move the casualty.
- [ ] Stay with them until help arrives.

Choking

- [ ] Ask 'Are you choking?' – if the casualty can reply, cough or breathe then it's mild – simply encourage them to cough.
- [ ] If they can't speak, cough or breathe, treat the incident as severe choking and deliver up to five back blows between their shoulder blades with the heel of your hand.
- [ ] Make sure these blows are hard enough to be effective. Previously guidance suggested giving back 'slaps', but research has shown that people weren't doing them with enough force. The change of terminology from 'slaps' to 'blows' is to emphasise the force with which you need to deliver them.
- [ ] If back blows fail, give up to five abdominal thrusts. Stand behind the casualty, place a clenched fist over the upper abdomen, grasp your fist with your other hand and pull inwards and upwards.

Poisoning

☐ Symptoms of poisoning vary depending on what and how much has been taken. Amongst young people, alcohol and other drugs, or the inhaled fumes of domestic chemicals such as deodorants, can be causes of poisoning.

☐ Look out for pain, vomiting and/or nausea, lethargy, loss of consciousness, convulsions and possible cardiac arrest.

☐ If you can, find out what's been taken. If you're not sure, give any medicines or tablets (or anything else that looks suspicious) to the ambulance crew.

☐ While waiting for the ambulance ensure that the airway is kept open.

☐ Unless you are explicitly told to do so by the emergency services, DON'T try to make the casualty vomit or take anything by mouth.

Chapter 6

Encouraging good behaviour

1 Introduction

With their teens pushing for more and more independence and spending more time outside the family, it may sometimes seem to parents that they are redundant. Not so. All evidence shows that, on the contrary, teens thrive when they maintain good relationships and have good communication with their parents.

Parents are able to rely on a younger child's acceptance of authority and discipline. Parents make major decisions about their child's life without consulting the child. Children are affectionate, generally eager to please and willing to help. Parenting a teenager requires a change of gear.

Teenagers, by contrast:

- [ ] are likely to challenge the opinions and views of adults
- [ ] will take their culture and many of their values from the peer group
- [ ] will expect to make more and more decisions for themselves, some of which will seem mistaken to their parents
- [ ] may respond aggressively or sullenly when freedoms are curtailed
- [ ] will frequently withdraw from the family, either to their bedrooms or to their peer group

Parents are no longer dealing with a child but with an emerging adult. Their parenting skills will need to be modified accordingly.

> There's nothing wrong with teenagers that reasoning with them won't aggravate

Tips for parents of teenagers

- [ ] Listen more – lecture, boss or tell less
- [ ] Respect their viewpoint even (especially) if it differs from yours
- [ ] Talk to your teen as an adult rather than a child
- [ ] Have it clear in your mind what is important – don't sweat the small stuff
- [ ] Set clear boundaries and stick to them
- [ ] As they mature, be prepared to modify the rules
- [ ] Make opportunities to spend time together and have fun
- [ ] Have faith in the work you have done to date and trust that your teenagers will (generally) do the right thing

Mum (calmly): 'What do you have to say for yourself?'

Emily first apologised for lying. Then told her mum that everyone else was going and she knew that if she asked to go, her mother would say 'No'.

Mum (picking up on the feeling): 'So you feel guilty about the lie. And do you think you are old enough to stay out all night?' (Not telling, but asking)

Emily admitted that she had done wrong to lie but then said: 'No, I don't think I am old enough to stay out all night but I do think you should allow me more freedom to go out at the weekend.'

At this point Emily's mother has got her to own up that she was in the wrong to lie and that she was not old enough to do what she did. Emily has now asked for more freedom at the weekend. All of this has been done without any shouting or tears.

Mum: 'You'd like more freedom at the weekends?' (showing she has listened and understood) 'What kind of things would you like to do that you are not allowed at the moment?'

Emily: 'There's a club for under-18s that finishes at 11pm. Could I go there?'

Mum: 'This is my view. You must never lie to me about where you are going and if it happens again there will be serious consequences. I have to know where you are, who you are with and that you are safe. I agree you are too young to stay out all night. I don't want you going to clubs where the average age is much older than you.' (Says what she thinks and how she feels) 'Let's talk about this under-18s club. Who else is going? How will you get home?'

And the conversation continues to a point at which both mother and daughter feel they have achieved something.

Some readers may feel that Emily should have been punished for what she did wrong. If her mother had punished her after this conversation, it would have felt justifiable and would have been accepted with good grace. Emily would have felt she did wrong, got found out and deserved to be punished. At the same time she has had a chance to apologise, get a new-won freedom and is trusted to behave better next time.

How to talk to a teenager

- ☐ Try not to get angry
- ☐ Be calm and respectful
- ☐ Don't lecture
- ☐ Don't criticise in them what you wouldn't criticise in others
- ☐ Try to see them as adults in the making
- ☐ Where there is disagreement, first listen then talk

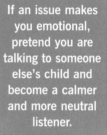

> If an issue makes you emotional, pretend you are talking to someone else's child and become a calmer and more neutral listener.

85

3 Boundaries, rules and limits

The art of parenting a teenager is to have clear rules about important matters, to be consistent in applying them, but to know when to modify them as the teenager moves through adolescence.

Teenagers want to take control of their own lives. Parents often feel anxious and try to retain their control, believing their teenagers are too young for the kinds of freedom they want. Conflicts of this type are most common between 13 and 16 years of age. Parents are often forced into more authoritarian measures to retain their control, while their teens get more frustrated at the restrictions on their freedom. Most teenagers want to stay friends with their parents and value their guidance. At the same time they want recognition that they are becoming adults.

Some guidelines for setting rules and establishing boundaries

■ **Adolescence is a training ground for the adult world**

Sooner or later teens will have to deal with the world without parental help. They will make the right choices if they are given the opportunity to become more responsible throughout their teenage years.

■ **Let go slowly, when you're confident that your teen is sufficiently mature**

It's easier to ease up when you have been too strict, than to try and withdraw a concession already granted.

■ **Make concessions**

If you say 'no' to everything you will only increase teenage rebelliousness. Listen, discuss and give a little and you will get credit for being flexible.

■ **Choose your battles**

Determine the things that matter – ease up on things that don't. Schoolwork is important, hairstyles are not.

■ **What is the peer group doing?**

If everyone else is allowed out unsupervised on Saturday afternoon, then perhaps you should let your 13-year-old go too. But if the peer group is doing things that you don't think your teen is ready for, stick to your principles.

■ **The best rules are those that are agreed with your teenagers**

Negotiate them. For example, if it's impossible to get them to keep their room tidy, make sure that they will at least agree to keep the 'public' areas, like the kitchen and sitting room, free of their debris.

■ **Give age-appropriate concessions**

If you continue to treat them as children, with too many petty rules and restrictions, they will turn away.

The three-step method for setting (and maintaining) boundaries

An example from www.raisingkids.co.uk

My 15-year-old son keeps invading my personal space. He will deliberately block my path, or his younger sister's, or he'll lean into our faces to exaggerate that he's listening. What is the best way to handle this? I've already tried ignoring it, telling him off, and talking generally about his conduct at a less stressful time.

This boy is literally and deliberately crossing boundaries by invading personal space. If he won't respond to his mother's reasonable approaches, then she should follow the three-step approach to setting boundaries:

1 State your position – using 'I' language – *eg* 'I don't like it when you stick your face into mine or block my path deliberately. I want you to stop doing it.' Make eye contact, speak in a firm voice, be clear and emphatic.

2 State the penalty he'll incur if he continues to cross the boundary – *eg* 'If you do it again, you will have your pocket money docked by £10' or 'You will not be allowed to go on the school trip.'

3 Most important, carry through – Don't back down or relent and give in when it comes time to exact the penalty. Don't give in to crying, whining, shouting or promises never to do it again. You must stick to your boundaries.

This simple three step procedure can be applied in a variety of situations. Some common flashpoints are covered in the remainder of this chapter.

4 Common flashpoints

Dress/make-up/tattoos/piercings

What should a parent do if their teenage son or daughter says they are going to get a tattoo or piercing? What if you don't like their choice of hairstyle or dress?

Pick your battle. Every generation has its own style, which frequently shocks the preceding generation. Dress and hairstyles are reversible and unlikely to result in any long-term damage, and are not issues to make a fuss about.

Tattoos (and to a lesser extent piercings, which leave a smaller but permanent hole in the skin) last for ever. Parents who disapprove of their teens getting tattooed have the law on their side until their teenager is 18: it's illegal in the UK to tattoo anyone under 18 without parental consent. They should make sure their teenager knows this.

Tattoos are permanent, so there is good reason to ensure that your teenager has thought it through. At some time in the future they may have cause to regret it – for instance, they may not want to be a pensioner at the swimming pool with a huge tattoo on their back. However, this argument is unlikely to be very effective with teenagers, who probably cannot imagine that they will ever be 60. The least you can do is try to persuade them not to have it in a very visible place.

If the teen is 18 or over parents have to accept that it's his/her body. Tattooing is not harmful if done properly and at this point the teen has the right to make the ultimate decision. But make sure they understand that tattoo removal is painful, expensive and not very effective.

Music/noise

Can't stand the music?

Music is central to the culture of teens. Different teenage tribes like different music, many of them being primarily defined by the artists and groups they follow. Parents who dislike the music are unlikely to be able to change their teenager's taste and will be wasting their time if they try. Parents may be shocked by the violent and misogynistic

> The main problem with teenagers is that they're just like their parents were at their age

lyrics of some music. However, listening to music like this won't cause a teenager to take on these attitudes and values. Parents should have faith in the values their teenagers learn at home.

Music too loud?

It's out of order to play music so loud that is affects other members of the family, or breaches the rules about public and private space. If the volume disrupts other people trying to do homework, read or watch television, then it crosses the boundary from teen space to family space. The neighbours are unlikely to be happy about it either. Encourage your teenager to use personal headphones but make sure the sound level isn't high enough to cause damage to their ears. As a rule, when headphones are being used at a safe level, the music can't be heard by anyone else at all.

Computer use

Some teenagers spend an excessive amount of time on the PC. Surfing and online game playing can become very addictive and adversely affect other aspects of a teenager's life. Signs to be worried about include:

- ☐ Declining standards of schoolwork
- ☐ Friends being neglected
- ☐ Staying up late into the night on the Internet
- ☐ Being very tired in the morning
- ☐ Skipping family meals and family events
- ☐ Eating at the computer

As always with teenagers, the most effective way to get agreement is by talking and getting them to agree to limit their use. Agree how much time homework should take – all schools give guidelines on this – and agree what is a reasonable bedtime. Then get a commitment not to rush homework just to get back to the computer. If matters become worse, remove temptation by taking away the computer cable so that it *can't* be used.

Sometimes a young person has to use the computer to complete their homework. Check that the assignments are completed at the end of the evening.

Unsuitable material

Unfortunately, there is a lot of unsuitable material online. To prevent teens from learning how to make a bomb or viewing pornography, the usual recommendation is that no young person should be allowed totally unsupervised access to the Internet. Problems arise because teens almost certainly know far more than their parents about computers and the Internet, which makes it very difficult for parents to supervise their use. However, some basic guidelines can be followed.

☐ Experts recommend that PCs be placed in family rooms where parents can monitor what their children are watching.
☐ It's possible to buy 'nanny' software to screen out offensive material; but be aware that computer-literate teens find it simple to override such programs.
☐ You control the means of access. Set clear rules – *eg* if they delete the browser history and passwords their Internet privileges will be withdrawn.
☐ Nothing beats getting to know the net yourself. Make time to familiarise yourself with current technology.

Chat rooms and bulletin boards

Most teenagers who have access to a computer will enter chat rooms and community sites, where teens can build an extended circle of virtual friends and share music and photographs. Even though this is an excellent way of connecting with other teens, it is open to abuse. Adults with ulterior motives enter chat rooms posing as teenagers, so take precautions:

☐ Young people should never give out personal information, addresses or telephone numbers online.

☐ They should never arrange to meet any online 'friend' offline without telling their parents.
☐ You should be aware that children in chat rooms use acronyms like 'PA' for Parent Alert to hide what's going on.

Other undesirable online activities

The anonymity of the Internet can lead young people into illegal activities that could hurt or harm others online. Posting false information, masquerading as someone else, creating websites aimed at ridiculing enemies, sending hate emails or 'cyber stalking' are against the law or will lead to trouble at school. Teenagers who breach copyright by posting pictures or text will have to pay up when found out.

Useful websites

The following sites have good advice on internet safety:
www.childnet-int.org
www.chatdanger.com
www.ncmec.org

Tidiness

One of the most common flashpoints between parents and their teenagers is the untidy bedroom. Mums who clear up after their teenage offspring find that far from being grateful the teens are annoyed that their space has been invaded!

Nagging a teenager about an untidy bedroom is exhausting and generally does not produce results. The room is unappealing, it's untidy, but it's not life-threatening. So forget about the mess – close the door and save your breath for more important arguments with your teenager.

House Rules

■ **Say what your minimum standards and rules are**

Make a distinction between their space and space that the family shares. A teenager's room is private space ('My room, my mess, my business'). Don't intrude, but make it clear that the rest of the house is everyone's space and different rules apply.

■ **Safety**

Is it a health hazard or fire risk? Smells, smoke or vermin will affect the whole family! Set clear boundaries, *eg* no smoking indoors, all food cleared up and binned, and lamps, hairdryers and straighteners kept in safe places to avoid the possibility of fire.

■ **Family space**

Work out rules they can accept which meet your minimum requirements. For example, in the kitchen, state clearly your expectation that when they have made something to eat they clean up after themselves (including the pots) and wipe down the surfaces. Stress that the kitchen is everyone's space and each person has the responsibility of keeping it clean.

■ **Don't give in and do it yourself**

Let them take the consequences of their untidiness. If your son can't find his football socks because they're still in the pile of clothing on the floor, then so be it. Consequences are the best teacher. They will appreciate what you do for them all the more when they realise the effort it involves to do it themselves.

Sex and staying overnight

It was the norm a generation ago to pretend that teenagers didn't have sex. Now some parents allow a teenage couple to share the same bed when at their house. Others insist on separate rooms.

Some things to think about if you are a parent facing this dilemma

■ **Times have changed**

Sixteen-year-olds do have sex and they do expect parents to accept it. It is difficult for many parents to recognise that their teenagers are sexual beings, especially if they make comparisons with their own youth. Ask yourself 'When will it be all right? When they are 18? 19? 21? Or only when they are married?

■ Concentrate on important issues

One of the best arguments for allowing teenagers to sleep together at home is that parents know where their son or daughter is, what they're up to, and with whom. If parents accept their children are having sex they can talk about vital issues like contraception and protection from sexually transmitted diseases (which have increased among 16 to 19-year-olds).

■ It's their home too

If you expect a young person to respect your family home, they also have the right to feel 'at home' there. Do you extend this right to mean they can bring a boyfriend or girlfriend home?

■ Set limits

There are limits and they will vary between households. It's the parents' home and they have a right to feel comfortable and expect certain standards of behaviour. Establish 'house rules' so that everyone feels comfortable, *eg* no breakfasting in pyjamas or dressing gowns. It's also best to explain that decisions are made in the light of a particular relationship. If parents fear that there may be a string of one-night stands, and that is unacceptable, they should make it clear from the start.

■ Finally...

Parents who can't accept it under their roof are entitled to refuse. However, they may feel obliged to explain their reasons and say at what age (if any) they would agree.

Boys and girls staying overnight together

It is very likely that at some point your teenager will ask to stay out at a friend's house where there will be other teenagers, both boys and girls. The fact that boys and girls are sleeping over together doesn't necessarily mean anything sexual – they are just mates.

Discovering secrets

Teenagers are notoriously secretive. There are whole parts of their lives that they hide from their parents, mostly because they fear their parents will not approve. This may be something harmless, like getting dressed at a friend's house because they know their parents won't approve of their clothing, but smoking, drinking and drug-taking are also usually kept secret. Similarly, when teenagers start having sex, especially if they are underage, they are unlikely to inform their parents first.

It often happens that parents find out about their teen's private life by seeing, reading or hearing something that was meant to be secret. When parents discover these secrets, especially if they do so by reading their teen's diary, letters, emails and texts, what should they do?

The problem here is how the parent found out. They crossed a boundary by prying into their teenager's private communications. This makes it very difficult to talk about the matter calmly, since the teenager will undoubtedly try to occupy the moral high ground and go on at length about the fact that their privacy has been violated.

What can parents do when faced with evidence that their teenager is engaging in dangerous or damaging behaviour?

■ Don't mention that they found out by reading a private diary, email or text

This will only muddy the waters. Avoid saying how you found out if at all possible.

■ The best advice is not to react immediately but try to calm down and think it through

The aim is to make sure that the young person is not engaging in dangerous behaviour, and, if you believe that they are, to help them see sense.

■ To have a full and frank discussion about a very emotional issue, one of you has to stay calm

■ **Ask neutral questions which make it possible to 'own up'**
For example:
♦ 'Are there boys/girls in your class who are sleeping with their girlfriends/boyfriends?'
♦ 'Have any of your friends been drunk?'
Followed by 'What about you, have you ever had too much to drink?

This is what psychologists call a 'When did you stop beating your wife?' question. It poses the question in a non-judgmental way, making it easier to confess to bad behaviour.

■ **Listen**
You need to be absolutely clear about what is going on, and the best way to find out is by not shouting or lecturing.

■ **If the problem is serious, you need to seek professional help**

Money and spending
With the onset of adolescence, children who previously only needed money for sweets, snacks and toys are now spending money 'going out', or on magazines, fashion accessories and clothing. They want to spend their 'own' money. At this point parents may increase the amount of pocket money they give to reflect changed circumstances. Some parents give their child an allowance that includesall their non-school-related expenditure.

An example of the kind of thing that occurs...
My 13-year-old is spending all her money on phone bills. How do I teach her to control her spending without taking away her independence?
Consequences are the best teacher. You won't teach teenagers to control their spending, if they know you will cough up the extra cash when they overspend. If you tell your teen that they have to pay their own way, that should make them stop and think. The bottom line is that people can't have something if they can't afford it. It's an important lesson to learn – especially in these days of easy credit.

If you plan to give your teenager an allowance, get them to make a budget and calculate what they have to buy and how much they will need. This is an opportunity for young people to learn about managing money.

5 Arguments

It is a lucky parent who gets through their child's adolescence without conflicts and arguments. When a flashpoint looms, try to keep these steps in mind:

■ Is it really worth fighting over?
If not, can you ignore it? With teenagers it's best to choose your battles.

■ Are you the right person to have this argument?
Sometimes a particular problem is so emotionally charged that it cannot be dealt with rationally. Some dads get furious when their little girl appears plastered with make-up, others can't tolerate smoking. If you know you'll find it hard to stay calm, try handing over to another person in the family who may have a different and more productive approach.

■ Stay calm
When you lose control in an argument and start shouting at each other, the possibility of sorting out the problem disappears. Things are often said in anger that are best left unsaid. Shouting makes it harder to listen, not easier.

■ Remember you're the adult
If you stay calm, it's more likely the other person will cool down. Getting angry just increases the volume.

■ Stick to the issue
Don't launch an all-out attack on your teen's appearance, behaviour or friends, as this may well cause the row to escalate out of control.

■ Are they trying to get a reaction?
If so, can you rise above it? Teens, like toddlers, are not above behaving badly to get your attention.

■ Try to offer choices instead of threats
For example, 'Would you like to have supper before or after you do your homework?'

■ Give explanations, not orders
Instead of saying 'You're coming to your Auntie Beryl's house and liking it,' try saying 'Auntie Beryl's too old to get out much now. She really looks forward to our visits.'

■ Avoid 'I told you so'
Don't feel you always have to be the winner. Sometimes you are right, but it's best not to say 'I told you so'. If, for instance, your teenager keeps their wallet in their back pocket and it's stolen, they will know it was a stupid thing to do and will appreciate the fact that you don't remind them.

■ Apologise
Don't be afraid to be the first to apologise, and always apologise if you are in the wrong. It's a good lesson for your teen to learn and will not undermine your authority. Equally, accept their apology (if they deign to make one!) with good grace, rather than responding with 'Oh yes! You're always sorry! I've heard that before...'

6 Mending a damaged relationship

What if the arguments just keep on coming? Maybe everyday interaction between parents and teenagers has descended into anger, criticism, distrust, and verbal abuse. When the atmosphere in the house is so poisonous, is it possible to put it right?

To get your relationship back to a more positive state, something has to change. You can't alter somebody else's behaviour unless they want to change. Nagging, lecturing, punishing or cajoling rarely work. A more effective strategy is trying to do things differently yourself. All parents can do is change their own behaviour and hope that their teenagers will change in response.

Changing your behaviour is often difficult

This is particularly true when the underlying feelings are deep-rooted. You may feel very hurt or angry, and have met with resentment and rejection at previous efforts to make up. Negative thoughts like 'Why should I put up with behaviour that I don't like?' or 'Why should I be the one to change, when it's their behaviour that's causing the problem?' can feed your anger.

Don't get stuck in this kind of thinking. If you want to build a better relationship, put these thoughts out of your mind. Anticipating a negative reaction usually encourages one.

Say, for example, you're irritated by your teen refusing to take off their headphones when you speak to them? Instead of your usual behaviour such as raising your voice, glaring, rolling your eyes or storming off, try writing a note saying 'Please take off your earphones, I would like to have a word with you.' Your instincts will cry out against this and you might justifiably feel you're pandering to your offspring, but someone has to act differently or the same scene will be played out over and over again. By deciding to take a different tack you're taking control of the situation rather than sticking in the rut.

'Fake it till you make it' is another strategy. Even if you feel the same, behave as if you feel differently. Ways of 'faking it' are:

■ Ignoring provocative behaviour
Walk away if your teen does something to wind you up. You may be seething inside, but if your teen sees that you're not there to react then they will see no point in provoking you.

■ Asking instead of telling
If they don't clean the bath after using it, don't order them to go up and do it NOW, ask politely.

■ Planning instead of reacting
If you feel you're always nagging your teenager to do their chores, why not give them a written list of jobs at the beginning of the week instead?

■ Catching your teen doing something right!
Find something positive to praise and acknowledge it instead of criticising. You may hate the clothes but can admire the trainers. This can be really effective if you praise specific things, however small, and knocks on the head the complaint, 'You're always criticising me!' or 'I never do anything right as far as you're concerned'.

◆ 'Well done for getting your homework completed on time.'
◆ 'You did an excellent job in putting that flat-pack cupboard together.'
◆ 'Thank you for helping me with the supper, I really appreciate it.'

You won't change your emotions overnight but you can start acting differently right now. Do it for long enough and you can get out of the vicious cycle and into a virtuous one.

This is a very difficult strategy to follow, especially if things have been bad for a long time, but it does work, so stick at it until you get results. Remember, the longer the relationship has been impaired, the longer it will take to change.

Change your tune

■ **Instead of complaining...**
'I don't know why I bother to clean this house, you're only going to mess it up again. As always.'

...ask for specific help
'It would be great if you could vacuum the sitting room and stairs, while I sort out the supper'

■ **Instead of slipping into the role of martyr...**
'I've spent two hours washing your dirty clothes.'

...try some benign neglect
'I'm sorry you can't find a clean shirt but it's up to you to sort out your own laundry.'

■ **Instead of nagging...**
'You know the coursework needs to be in by Monday – why aren't you working?'

...try motivating
'The new game you want is released on Saturday. If you've done your assignment by then, why don't we go shopping for it together at the weekend?'

■ **Instead of getting angry...**
'It's the third time this week I've prepared dinner and you haven't turned up'

...get even
'I'm busy most days this week, so you'll have to get your own food. There's plenty in the freezer.'

7 Building a sense of responsibility

Teens are quick to claim the rights and freedoms of adults, but what about adult responsibilities? A major task for parents is to prepare their teenagers to accept more responsibility. This includes caring for themselves, for their surroundings, for their family and for friends. In the wider sense it involves finding work, concentrating on schoolwork and managing money.

What responsibilities?
The following can all be undertaken by anyone over the age of 12:

- ☐ Keeping their own room clean
- ☐ Making simple food for themselves
- ☐ Keeping the kitchen and family space tidy
- ☐ Helping prepare the family meal
- ☐ Sorting and (later) doing their own laundry
- ☐ Walking the dog, cleaning up after pets
- ☐ Organising kit for school
- ☐ Planning homework
- ☐ Spending and saving pocket money sensibly
- ☐ Doing chores around the house or getting a weekend job for extra cash

Get your teenager to agree with you that these responsibilities are fair and reasonable, and are things that they are capable of actually doing – *eg* make sure they know how to use the washing machine properly and how to sort their laundry before you expect them to do their own washing.

There is no reason why a working parent should come in from a full day's work to find a teenager lolled in front of the television waiting to be fed. Take into account homework and other demands on their time. When tasks are successfully completed, make sure you let them know how much you appreciate it!

8 Problem solving

Rushing to help when things go wrong sends out the message that Mum or Dad will always come to the rescue. It's hard to watch someone struggle when you know you can put things right, but without the opportunity to work things through it's impossible to learn how to solve problems.

'Active listening' is one of the most effective ways to encourage problem-solving skills. The 'active listening' technique helps a young person confront their own feelings, and once they have taken this step they're on their way to understanding of their own emotions and developing emotional intelligence. Bringing a worry out into the open is the first step in dealing with it. From this point you can help them face the problem and perhaps find a solution to it.

For example, if there's a problem with coursework

■ Understand the problem

Perhaps the teacher hasn't explained the assignment fully or they can't get the books out of the library. Are they finding the topic difficult or are they struggling to catch up after missing a few classes? Useful information can be wrapped in angry or critical comments, so try to ignore sniping or swearing and let them keep going until they are finished.

■ Pick up on any feelings

For example, you could say something like 'Are you worried that you will fail if you can't get the right books in time?'

■ What's the goal? Brain-storm for solutions

Having understood the problem and the associated feelings, the next step is to agree the goal. In this case, the project has a deadline which can't be missed. A way of reaching the goal has to be found, without the books from the library.

■ Write down all the possibilities

List all the options for completing the project. Is the book available anywhere else? In another library? Amazon? Can the relevant bits be photocopied in the library? Is the information from the internet? A concrete list shows you are taking the problem seriously. Give equal weight to all the suggestions. At this stage don't eliminate any solution, no matter how daft it seems.

■ Turn the ideas into action

Discuss which solutions are practical and then put them into action, bearing in mind that some of the alternatives will take more time than others. Don't explore only one solution, when there is a tight deadline, it is best to cover several options.

Teaching problem solving and working through issues together will encourage a young person to sort things out for themselves in the longer term. At first you'll probably have to offer a lot of input. Be supportive, but don't intervene or take the problem away. Allow space for them to make mistakes. It is only by confronting and working through problems that adolescents learn for themselves.

Chapter 7

Family matters

(family changes, siblings, step-families)

1 Becoming less family-orientated

Unlike their younger siblings, adolescents are no longer dependent on the family for all of their physical and emotional needs. Teenagers need to separate from the family so that they can develop their own individual personalities. When most young people come through the rebellious phase to enjoy a strong relationship with their families, they are doing so out of choice and not from necessity.

2 ...but still part of the family unit.

Putting some emotional (or even physical) distance between themselves and the family is a step in the process of maturing, but space doesn't have to mean exclusion.

If you're looking for other ways to strengthen the family bond, the following ideas are worth a try – bear in mind that all teenagers are individuals and approaches that work for some young people may put others off!

■ Keep a few predictable 'rituals'
...such as watching a favourite TV programme together on Friday evenings or eating Sunday lunch together. Routine events can be calming and reassuring when everything else is unpredictable.

■ Show that you value their new skills and abilities
Ask your teenager to help you with a grown-up task (eg installing a wireless network in the home, or sharing a long-distance drive) or recommend their services to a friend.

■ Make their friends feel included

■ Give them as much space as possible within the home
A young person who feels their privacy is respected at home won't always be so eager to be elsewhere.

■ Let them choose a day trip or activity they enjoy, that the entire family can participate in

■ Look out for shared interests
Are there any sports or creative classes you could attend together?

■ Schedule regular one-on-one time together
Go out for a walk or have a meal together.

3 Separation and divorce

They may seem mature, but teens often take the break-up of their family home very badly. Young people may blame one or both parents and can be very censorious if a third party is involved. They may fantasise about getting their parents back together again.

Some guidelines for telling teenagers
Make your decisions privately and definitely. Your children will have been aware that something is wrong, and letting them know that the situation is final will help them avoid futile or desperate efforts to 'make things better'. It may even come as a relief of a sort.

■ **Let them express their feelings, even if it makes you feel guilty and defensive**

■ **There are some issues your teens don't need to know about, such as money, property, or other relationships**

Unless they ask you directly don't raise these topics, which frequently lead to bitterness and resentment.

■ **Deal with the practical questions that should be dealt with among all of you and give straight answers**

'Where will we live?' 'Who will we live with?' 'What about school?' Young people may have fears about the effect of the divorce on their standard of living: 'Will I still be able to go on holiday? To university? Will we have to move to a smaller house?' Decide these things between you in advance. Don't fight about them in front of the children.

■ **Don't make your teen your confidant**

Teenagers may seem old enough to confide in, they may even accept the news calmly and not appear upset, but beware of overloading them emotionally. It's difficult to bottle up the hurt and rejection you may feel, but talk to your own friends about this and not your children. You are the adult and should resist burdening your teenagers with your pain. They have their own feelings to deal with and need support from you.

■ **Don't turn them against their other parent**

Remember you are the one who divorced, not your children, who love you both and won't want to take sides. After a painful separation, staying in touch with both parents is very important, especially during the adolescent years. It's easy to feel secretly pleased that your ex is being 'punished' by your children, but in the longer term freezing Mum or Dad out can mean that teenagers suffer the loss of a parent along with all the other losses. You can help them by saying explicitly that you want them to make it up with their parent and that they don't have to prove their love for you by taking sides.

■ **Don't lean on your children for emotional support**

After divorce adolescents may feel they have to support the parent they live with, by taking on responsibilities in the home, both practical but also emotional. This is particularly true for young males. ('I'm the man of the house now') When a boy is dealing with the difficulties of becoming an adult, feeling responsible for a parent is an additional burden.

■ **Choose your time to introduce a new partner**

Accepting a step-parent or new partner can feel disloyal, especially if that individual is seen to be the cause of the break-up. When a parent leaves a marriage, children feel physically and emotionally abandoned, and teenagers, especially during early adolescence, tend to see things in terms of black and white. One parent may be seen as the injured party, with the other cast in the role of villain.

■ **Discourage them from saying critical things about your ex**

Stress that although you and your partner have split up, their feelings for the other parent won't change. Whatever your ex's faults, he or she is still your children's father or mother. What happened is just between the two of you, so make sure your teenagers know you believe it is important for them to have a relationship with both of their parents.

Divorce handled well can be a lesson in how to manage the changes life brings, and you can set a good example of how to manage conflict. Teenagers whose parents have divorced on good terms can learn to approach difficulties with courage and optimism, and often have stronger relationships with their siblings. They may learn to see problems as challenges which – although hurtful and unsettling – can be resolved.

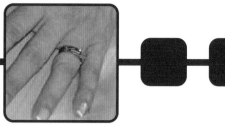

4 Parent's new partner

You chose your new partner, the rest of the family didn't. Now a new adult has come into the household and there's very little teenagers can do about it. The reactions of a typical teen will be very complex:

■ Jealousy
The feeling that there is a competition between them and your new partner, especially if that partner is of the same sex as they are. If you have previously been a one-parent family you are all the more precious to your children and jealousy can be more intense. Your new partner is a rival for your love.

■ Anger
Loss of a parent through death or divorce can lead to feelings of being abandoned and anger at the departed parent. These feelings may be directed at the step-parent who 'replaces' the lost parent.

■ Unfavourable comparisons
A step-parent may be constantly compared to the 'perfect' absent parent. It's a common fantasy that every difficulty in life would vanish if only mum or dad came back.

The relationship between a teen and a stepfather or stepmother can become really stressful during adolescence. A classic emotional triangle develops, with the parent torn between two people with equal claim on their affections and attention. Persistent conflict between parent and child can put the relationship between the adults in the family in jeopardy.

'You're not my dad'
Step-parents, especially if they have been in the family for a long time, will naturally take on the role of the parent with a stroppy teenager. Much as teenagers resent their parents criticising them, forbidding them to do things they want to do, and curtailing their freedom, they resent it many times more when it comes from a step-parent.

A step-parent who has been in loco parentis for several years, who has supported the teen emotionally and financially, will feel angry and rejected when told 'You've no right to tell me anything, you're not my dad/mum'. The fact that the relationship has been good for many years doesn't mean that adolescence won't put it under extreme stress. It is possible that angry feelings that weren't expressed years earlier may now emerge.

A step-parent who steps back and doesn't try to interfere may nevertheless get drawn into the conflict between partner and stepchild, when the teenager is disrespectful, rude or abusive to his partner.

The adult relationship may suffer as a result. The natural parent may resent the interference of the step-parent and the step-parent may be angry with the natural parent for not being stricter with the rebellious teenager.

Guidelines to managing the relationship
■ For the natural parent:
◆ *When your new partner appears on the scene, it takes time for everyone to get to know each other. While you may love your children don't expect that your partner will feel the same way, and while you love your partner don't expect the children to feel the same way. Peaceful co-existence and mutual respect is enough to hope for in the beginning, although warmer and more affectionate feelings may follow in time.*

◆ *As with any major change, give as much notice as possible and let your teenagers have time to adjust. Even if they like your new partner, upheaval is still stressful! If your partner is moving in, have realistic expectations and give everyone time to settle down. Remember that if your new partner is moving into your home, your kids will feel very territorial and won't want to give up their space – and that may include the chair they always sit in when watching television.*

♦ If there are specific things about the new set-up that bother your teenager, hear them out and see if you can work out a solution. Don't automatically defend you partner to your teen, nor your teen to your partner. You will be playing referee for quite some time and their complaints won't always be well-founded.

♦ When the inevitable rows blow up, setting limits on the expression of feelings can stop things getting out of hand and people saying things that shouldn't be said. If your child criticises your partner, reacting angrily will only make them feel you are taking your partner's side and increase the sense of competition.

♦ Feelings of dislike and jealousy towards your partner will only dissipate if worked at over time, but behaviour is something else and can be changed immediately. Make it clear that living together is something that everyone has to work at and that certain kinds of behaviour are not allowed – for example, rudeness or aggression.

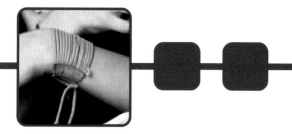

For the new partner:

♦ *Teens don't want a new mum or dad. Attempts to take on the role of the absent father or mother can be a big cause of resentment, especially if you try to be the disciplinarian.*

♦ *You're the adult. You have probably gone through many transitions in your life, whereas a teenager has limited experience of change. Teens are going through a major physical, social and emotional upheaval of their own, and the parts of their brain that make sensible decisions are not yet fully developed. Cut them some slack and don't get involved if you can avoid it, especially if it's not a major issue.*

♦ *Support your partner and don't criticise the decisions they make, even if you disagree with them. Be there as a listening ear and give your own opinion, but once the decision is taken support it.*

♦ *Try to find things you can all do together and enjoy, like taking walks, watching football and playing board games. Aim at being a friend and a support to the young person in the household and keep some distance between you.*

♦ *On a more positive note, teenagers in search of a same-sex role model and guide may find their step-parent just the person to step into this position.*

5 Mum's having a baby

Teens don't want to think about parents having sex – and now the reality is being forced on them! What will their friends say? How will it change their lives? A new sibling is quite a different proposition for a teenager than it is for a toddler or pre-teen. Gauging how an older – possibly wiser – teenager will react to the news calls for forethought. It really depends on the individual.

The news may come as a shock at first but don't anticipate a negative reaction. Some girls are already becoming maternal at this age, and even boys are developing a soft streak for little kids – teens often end up secretly excited, and a tiny baby isn't a threat to their status as a 'senior' member of the family.

Tell your teenagers before the world knows

Bear in mind that they are quick on the uptake. It's especially important if you're suffering from morning sickness or feeling very tired – one worried teenager's unexpected reaction to the announcement of a forthcoming sibling was 'Thank God for that, I thought you were dying!' It's better that the news comes from you rather than via someone else, so tell them before they hear it from others.

A forthcoming baby in the household is usually the last thing a teenager expects to deal with, so understand that they may be taken aback. An obvious sign of parental fertility (and everything that goes with it) is not what most teens are ready for. Your child will probably be unsure about how to feel or act. Part of them may feel excited at the news, while another part is anxious and concerned.

A new baby can be reassuring, as it makes it clear that a young person's parents are very clearly still 'together'. If it's a step-sibling it can be more upsetting. Does it mean you'll love them less? Will you devote all your time to your new family? As a parent, especially if it's your first baby with your new partner, you will be readjusting to your new relationships too. Amidst the many distractions, find time to listen to your teenagers.

6 Family relocating

The ability to create relationships quickly and easily is a valuable life-skill and relocation is an opportunity for teenagers to start acquiring it. Unfortunately, young adults can miss their school and friends badly. If you're concerned about your teens feeling lonely and isolated, encourage them to stay in contact by text messages, email and phone calls, which are all easy and (relatively) cheap ways of staying in touch. Invite old friends to stay too.

Teenage years are a difficult time to move. Lack of confidence and growing self-consciousness make it difficult to make friends in the easy way they could when they were younger.

If possible, schedule the move to coincide with the time that children change schools (at 16, for example) or get separated up into sets (at the beginning of the GCSE course). This way your teen won't be the only 'new starter'. Established peer groups often reform during such periods as different pupils follow different subjects. Before starting at a new school, talk to the year tutor – explain the situation and ask them to help your teen settle in. The teacher may be able to suggest extra-curricular activities for them to get involved in, or set them up with another student to do projects together.

7 Step-siblings

While a parent and new partner have steadily built up an emotional bond, the kids from the two families have not fallen in love with each other. For teenagers, the closeness demanded in a shared household comes suddenly and may not be welcome.

■ Understand the feelings

In step-families, the stresses of ordinary family life are multiplied, especially in the early days. A new stepbrother or stepsister can be seen as an invader, particularly if they move into the family home. Step-siblings come together with different expectations, family habits and rules. Jealousy can erupt over issues of space, possessions, and age differences. Until a new way of living together develops these conflicts are almost inevitable.

■ The resident enemy

Busy lives and a growing burden of responsibilities cause a build-up of tension that must be released. This often happens at home and step-siblings are a ready-made target for attack in such situations.

■ If you've ever shared a house, remember how difficult flatmates can be?

And you usually have some say in choosing a flatmate – but your teenagers had no choice in their new step-siblings.

■ Settle for peace, not love

Listen to both sides, not only your own teenager's story. When you think you understand the basis of their (probably mutual) dislike, call a family meeting to discuss the situation.

■ Don't criticise, work out a solution together

The most important thing here is to ban all name-calling, criticising and other negative behaviour. Insist that since they live under the same roof, they must find a way of living together. Get them to list the things that cause the most friction. Ask them to choose the two or three that cause the most arguments, and find a way of resolving these problems.

■ Present a united front

Despite your natural inclinations, you and your partner must at all costs avoid getting drawn into the conflict. Adolescents are very perceptive and may find that needling their step-siblings is an excellent means of creating tension between you and your partner. Though you may act as impartial referees, the onus is on them to resolve their differences.

8 Illness and bereavement

Only a few fortunate people get through their teenage years without encountering death or serious illness. Although the deaths of grandparents and older relatives may occur, sadly your teen may also have to deal with the death of a school friend or even a younger family member. Remember that teens are often very sensitive and the death of a pet – or even a famous person who they admire – can have an impact. There are many excellent and detailed sources of information about handling adolescent bereavement and this section is therefore intended as no more than a very short introduction.

Death or serious illness in the family can be particularly traumatic for teenagers. They are struggling with their own transition from child to adult, they are at a stage where they are questioning previously received ideas, and their relationships are more complex than in childhood.

For example, a young child may grieve over a grandparent's death, but a sorrowful teenager may also be assaulted by a mixture of emotions including:

☐ Guilt ('Why didn't I visit Granny more often?')
☐ Relief ('I hated to see her suffering. I'm glad it's over')
☐ Anger ('She was such a kind person. Why did she have to die like that?')
☐ Fear ('Will that happen to me when I get older?')
☐ Obligation ('I need to be strong for my family')
The Child Bereavement Trust (**www.childbereavement.org.uk**) finds that teenagers' needs at times of bereavement are:

☐ To have trustworthy adults around to talk to
☐ To have their feelings received without judgement or criticism
☐ To be allowed to cry or express their grief when they feel able to
☐ To be accepted when their grieving doesn't fit conventional patterns *eg* when tears don't flow at the funeral
☐ To be able to express anger and other feelings in a secure setting

If the death has happened within the family, parents will be going through their own personal grieving process and be at a low ebb themselves. Your teenager needs to be able to vent their sorrow and their feelings of vulnerability and helplessness at a time when the adults around them are preoccupied with their own feelings. Intense and difficult feelings may arise at the most unexpected times and it is helpful to have someone outside of the family to talk to as well.

Useful websites
www.childbereavement.org.uk
www.crusebereavementcare.org.uk
www.samaritans.org

Samaritans > Confidential emotional support 24 hours

http://www.samaritans.org/

Apple (84) ▾   Amazon   eBay   Yahoo!   News (770) ▾

SAMARITANS

DO YOU NEED SOMEONE TO TALK TO?   CAN YOU OFFER US YOUR SUPPORT?   WOULD YOU LIKE TO KNOW MORE?

We don't know when people might need Samaritans.
That's why we're here 24 hours a day.

Make a date
24:7
WITH SAMARITANS

FIND YOUR LOCAL BRANCH

CALL US
UK: 08457 90 90 90
ROI: 1850 60 90 90

WRITE TO US
Chris, P.O. Box 9090
Stirling, FK8 2SA

EMAIL US
Jo@samaritans.

© Samaritans 2007. Samaritans is a registered charity, number: 219432 Terms & Conditions | Privacy statement

9 Squabbling siblings

It's normal for siblings to fight over everything and anything, even when they reach their teens. Sibling conflict and disagreements are facts of life. When peace finally breaks out between brothers and sisters it's because they have used problem-solving and negotiation skills instead of fighting. These skills are very useful when they have to deal with other people at school, at work and in adult life.

Identifying the triggers can help you deal with them and enjoy a quieter life. Look at what's behind the fighting:

■ What's the usual motive?

Older children come to assume that they have certain rights because of their age. They may like to boss the younger child and be the leader at everything. This works fine with an easy-going younger sibling or if there is a large age gap. With a small age gap or a more assertive sibling, the older child's supremacy will be challenged, sometimes with fists. Between step-siblings, any attempt at bossing, ordering or telling will be rejected.

■ Deal with the things that cause the most persistent fights

If it's about possessions, make them establish rules about sharing. If it's about space, let them divide their shared space in an agreed way. Don't you introduce the rules, make them work it out for themselves. That way they are more likely to stick to it.

■ What are the times and triggers?

Do your teens seem to fight more at the end of the day, when they are tired and irritable, or are they edgy in the morning? Plan activities to help them stay on an even keel. Watching television in the evenings (avoiding violent and aggressive programmes), playing on the computer or listening to music are all suitable low-key activities. For anyone who is irritable in the morning, simply don't engage with them.

■ Is it caused by personality clashes?

Sometimes the individual personalities of brothers and sisters make it difficult for them to get along together. You can't alter the way they react to each other, but you should explain how disturbing it is for the rest of the family. Tell them everybody else wants a quiet life. Ask them to sort out their disagreements and agree a workable compromise. You may have to act as referee at first but

eventually you should be able to trust them to do it on their own.

Tactics to beat bickering between teenage siblings

■ Instigate a penalty system

Give them a warning that if they aren't being civil to each other – or at least quiet – then they will have to get off the computer, phone or whatever is causing the problem. The football metaphor, 'You're on a yellow card!', is a graphic way to issue a warning and works particularly well with boys. Fear of the subsequent 'red card' and 'sending off' may be just enough to stop them bickering.

■ Taking it outside

Bickering and squabbling often bothers the listener more than the antagonists. Faced with low-level warfare of the most irritating kind, try moving the battlefield to somewhere where innocent bystanders can't hear them. As long as you're sure that no one will get hurt, this solves your problem.

■ Separate them

If the bickering starts again, separate them. If they can't get along together, they'll have to be alone.

■ Let them solve their own problems

If you want them to sort out the cause of the problem, different tactics are required. Tell them they have a certain amount of time to get the matter sorted, after which you'll turn off the DVD or games console, or remove whatever is causing the disagreement. The best long-term solution to squabbling and bickering is to help young people develop their own ways of settling their differences. Reaching a compromise provides excellent lessons in negotiating and problem-solving. When the agreement breaks down – as it undoubtedly will – make them go back and work things out again.

10 Sibling rivalry

Is it safe to assume that over-competitive teenage siblings will grow out of it? Envy and rivalry can emerge during adolescence when insecurities are keenly felt. It's often the eldest who may feel threatened and challenged in areas they used to be 'best at'. It's pretty galling to have your younger brother or sister come out with the answer before you've had a chance to think about the question!

First-borns get used to being best at everything. As children get older, difference in their ages matters less and the younger ones start to develop their skills and talents. Is the 'baby'

catching up with – maybe surpassing – an older sibling?

What lies behind the competitive behaviour?

Complaints reveal the feelings underneath, so if the eldest feels they've lost 'prime position' look out for comments like 'You think you're better than everyone' or 'You're such a know-all'. One sibling may belittle another's achievements ('Anyone could do that') or avoid competing where victory is not guaranteed.

Try these tactics for neutralising competitive behaviour:

■ Look at all their achievements, not just academic success

Don't over-emphasise the importance of academic achievement. Many young people feel less able than their siblings because they don't do as well at school. Children compare with each other. They make judgements about which talents and abilities are important based on what their parents say. If your children feel that being clever is the most important measure of someone's worth, then they may feel less worthy if they are less clever. Cleverness is only one talent of many. Unfortunately, for children it's often the one that seems most important, because they spend so much of their time at school. School is only one area of life and shouldn't be the only measure by which they determine their self-worth.

■ Identify their special qualities

Is he or she practical, creative, good at sport, a natural organiser, or a great socialiser? Being aware of their strengths and developing their confidence in their

own unique abilities takes away the need for competition. Make sure they understand that – though different – their talents are equally valued.

■ Discourage high-achievers from gloating

■ Don't expect too much
Are your expectations of the first-born too high? It's easy to overestimate the maturity of the eldest.

■ Never make comparisons between them
Young people should feel that they are valued for themselves, as unique individuals who have special qualities and talents. A comparison is always a put-down for one of the people involved – it's likely to make them worse and it drives a wedge between your children. Get into the habit of looking at the individual's behaviour, without any reference to their siblings.

■ Don't compare directly
Saying 'Why can't you be more like your sister?' won't motivate the 'bad' sibling to become more like the 'good' one. This rarely happens. A more likely outcome is that each of them becomes confirmed in their roles, the 'good girl' and the 'bad boy'.

■ Don't compare indirectly
Comparisons favourable to one sibling should also be avoided, since it is an implied criticism of the other. If you say 'You always look neat and tidy,' the implication 'unlike your sister or brother' is clear to everyone. Don't try to make them feel good by highlighting the shortcomings of their sibling. Avoid saying things like, 'You're so cheerful, unlike your sister who's always complaining.' It encourages rivalry and undermines the relationship between them. Try instead to work with your children to build positive and supportive relationships between them.

 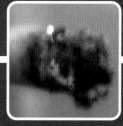 

Chapter 8

Damage-limitation strategies

1 Drinking

Some families only use alcohol socially – *eg* champagne at a christening – others enjoy moderate drinking at home with meals, and others abstain for religious reasons. Some families have issues with drink because of their family history. The way in which you approach your teenager's attitude to alcohol very much depends on your family background.

Some facts about underage drinking:

☐ 10 per cent of 12 to 15-year-old drinkers say they buy their own alcohol; 66 per cent of 15-year-olds have bought booze.

☐ 48 per cent of 15-year-old boys and 40 per cent of 15-year-old girls have had a drink in any week. 84 per cent of 12-year-olds have drunk alcohol. By the age of 16, 94 per cent of young people have tried it.

☐ 33 per cent of 15-year-olds drink alcohol in a bar at least once a week and 52 per cent of 15-year-olds say they either drink at home or at a friend's house.

☐ Over 5 per cent of 14 to 15-year-olds, and just under 10 per cent of 15 to 16-year-olds drink beyond the recommended maximum limits of regular consumption.

☐ 10 per cent of underage drinkers have been either too hung over to go to school the next day, have needed a drink in the morning, or have got into trouble at school as a result of drinking.

☐ 40 per cent of 13 and 14-year-olds were 'drunk or stoned' when they first had sex.

If you find the idea of your teenager drinking alcohol particularly upsetting because of your beliefs, your religious leader will probably be able to help. It's inevitable that they will have come across this problem before and will have experience in tackling it.

Drinking is very common amongst under-18s, despite the fact that they are below the legal age for drinking. Many parents feel uneasy about underage drinking and concerned about how to deal with it. If your child is drinking regularly and to excess and is possibly engaging in dangerous activities, you need professional help. Help for parents is available from Al-Anon (**www.al-anonuk.org.uk**); teenagers can find help at **www.thesite.org**.

If a 16-year-old socialises with a group of friends who like to visit pubs, clubs and wine bars, should responsible parents be letting them go? Are parents being too strict by forbidding it, when all their friends regularly visit clubs and pubs? If teens are forbidden to do what their peer group is doing, will they inevitably lose their friends?

These are problems for many parents who are happy to allow their teens out in the evening but not happy about where they go. In dealing with these issues, parents have to consider the legal, social and health implications of underage drinking.

The law relating to drinking and teenagers

Under-14s may only be in the bar of licensed premises at licensee's discretion and if accompanied by an adult. Under-16s may be present in a restaurant etc where alcohol is served with a meal and at the licensee's discretion may consume (but not purchase) alcohol bought by a parent or guardian

Over-16s may purchase beer, porter, cider, or perry with a meal in an eating area on licensed premises (In Scotland wine also) but may not purchase or be supplied with or consume alcohol in a bar.

Police have powers to confiscate alcohol from under 18s drinking in public and to contact their parents. Licensees and staff of licensed premises have a positive duty not to sell alcohol unless they are reasonably certain that the purchaser is not under the age of 18.

It is, however, legal for someone over 14 to be in licensed premises as long as they are not buying or drinking alcohol.

Social aspects

One of the most important things at this age is the peer group. If a teenager's friends are nice kids who work hard at school and are well behaved, then you can relax a little. Unfortunately, the pub is where a lot of teen social life is these days. Many 16-year-olds will try to go to bars and pubs to drink. They will rely on looking older than their years and hope that they won't be challenged by the bar staff. If all the rest of the group are going, it is unlikely that one member will opt out.

The parents' main aim should be to get across the message of responsible drinking. Avoid lecturing and try to engage in a discussion; for example, how much alcohol is too much, what kinds of pubs and clubs are their teens going to and what kind of other people go there? Make sure that you know where your teen is, who they are with, and what time they are coming home.

When young people see moderate drinking at home, it will be those attitudes to alcohol which prevail in the long run. In the short run, you may see signs of teenage excess occasionally but that goes with the territory of parenting a teenager.

Health

The amount of alcohol a person consumes is measured in units. As a rule, health experts recommend that adult men drink no more than 21 units per week. Adult women shouldn't exceed 14 units per week. A unit is equal to:
- [ ] Half a pint of beer or cider
- [ ] A small glass of wine
- [ ] A single measure of spirits (eg whisky, vodka, rum or gin)

Personal safety guidelines for young people
- [ ] Never drink and drive
- [ ] Don't get into a car if the driver has been drinking (especially if it is a young person who has only recently passed their test)
- [ ] Make sure you know how much alcohol is too much for you, regardless of how much your friends knock back
- [ ] Avoid drinking competitions, and if you feel pressured to drink more than you want to, go home
- [ ] Stay with friends and don't go off alone or with someone you don't know (call a cab home if you need to)
- [ ] Beware of drinks that may be spiked – either with drugs or more alcohol (inexperienced drinkers are unlikely to be able to taste the difference between a triple vodka-and-orange and a single)

See Chapter 5 for what to do in the event of acute alcoholic poisoning.

What if a young person's drinking is getting out of hand?

If you notice some of the following alcohol-related problems, this can be a sign that social drinking is becoming something more dangerous:

- [ ] Relationship problems triggered by drink
- [ ] Risk-taking behaviour, *eg* 'dare-devil' climbing, provoking fights, or walking home alone
- [ ] Embarrassing public behaviour, especially if they find it hard to stop drinking despite being distressed by their behaviour
- [ ] Getting into trouble with the police
- [ ] Physical signs such as bloating, a red face, internal problems with kidneys or liver
- [ ] Dependency issues such as needing a drink to overcome shyness or before going to social events

Young individuals drink for different reasons. Concerned parents may find it helpful to discuss the problem both together and with health professionals before talking to their teenager.

Useful websites

Possible sources of advice are Al-Anon (020 7403 0888, **www.al-anonuk.org.uk**), for families of people with drinking problems; Alcohol Concern (020 7928 7377, **www.alcoholconcern.co.uk**); and Drinkline (a free, confidential helpline) on 0800 917 8282.

TheSite.org (**www.thesite.org**) aims to be the first place all young adults turn to when they need support and guidance through life. It's owned and run by YouthNet UK, a registered charity.

2 Smoking

The first sign that a teenager is smoking is often when their parents come across their cigarettes! Bad breath, a persistent cough, and a general smell of smoke can also be indicators that your teen has taken up the habit. With the new anti-smoking regulations, the excuse of hanging out in a smoky cafe has gone. Short-term smoking is unlikely to do much damage unless your teenager is careless with a lit cigarette. The most important thing is to try to prevent smoking becoming a long-term habit.

Discuss the reasons your teenager smokes – is it to conceal shyness, reduce appetite, aid concentration, to feel a sense of belonging? If you can help them work out alternative strategies the need to smoke may vanish.

Point out how expensive smoking is and get your teenager to work out the cost of smoking ten cigarettes a day for ten years! The figure may well be enough to shock them into stopping.

Smoking can be anti-social in unexpected ways. Does your child want to make asthmatic friends feel uncomfortable? Is it really a good idea to be the person diving outside every 20 minutes for a fag?

Bribery can work too, although it's best kept as a last resort. Some parents promise a lump sum of money on their child's 21st birthday provided they haven't taken up smoking.

3 Drugs

Most young people will encounter drugs at some point before their 18th birthday. Communication and an open attitude is vital, and beginning to discuss some of the issues when your child is still relatively young (perhaps before they go up to senior school) can help to keep them talking to you later on.

A few tips for talking about drugs to teenagers:

☐ If you want to be a credible source of help and advice to your teen, first get all the information yourself, so that you know what you are talking about. Most parents have no idea about the drug scene – certainly they know less than their children – so their admonitions and threats lack credibility. You may have smoked pot as a teenager, but nowadays 'skunk' – a much stronger version grown from specially cultivated seeds – is more common. Twenty years ago smoking pot was likely to make you giggly, hungry and perhaps slightly dizzy, whereas skunk is more likely to cause hallucinogenic effects, and carries a bigger risk of anxiety, panic and paranoia. Drug services do not just offer help to teenagers, they are also there for parents who need support and will be happy to answer any of your questions or offer suggestions about tackling difficult topics.

☐ Avoid discussing your own behaviour. Your experience is NOT what your child is doing now, no matter how up-to-date you think you are – your 'norm' is not theirs. You can empathise with your teenager without needing to say you did the same thing. Some teenagers may think a parent's admission of drug use is a 'green card' and most young people will store the knowledge up to use against you in a future argument. It's natural for teenagers to go against their parents – discussing your own drug experiences is a dangerous gamble and can backfire.

☐ Many young people don't want to talk to their

parents about drugs but will talk to other people. Try to see this as normal teenage behaviour rather than rejection.

☐ Make sure they know where to go for information.

☐ Talk about legal 'drugs' as well as illegal ones – smoking, alcohol, caffeine (especially energy drinks) and diet pills.

If a serious problem ever develops, remember that it will always be down to more than drugs. It will not necessarily be down to parents either! Look out for early signs that something is bothering your child – it could be a problem with school, friends, his/her environment, or even your teenager's mental disposition.

Keep in mind that though you can offer advice and support to a young person they may not accept it. Some encouraging research has shown that when they feel they need help, most young people will go to the person who offered that help in the first place.

If you think your teenager is using drugs, it can be very upsetting and shocking. There are a lot of scare stories surrounding drugs, and while some of these are justified there are different levels of use and related dangers. Try to take time out, think things through calmly, and find out the facts before you intervene. Drug counsellors use five key questions when discussing a client's experience, that can help you both when assessing the situation and talking to your teenager:

☐ What?
☐ Why?
☐ When?
☐ Where?
☐ How?

When you come to discuss drugs with your teenager, start with a non-judgemental attitude. Don't push for details but be open and receptive, and remember that it's normal for teenagers to experiment, whether in terms of music, sports or drugs. Your role is to keep them away from long-term harm.

Useful websites
You can find information about drugs on various websites, which can offer parents excellent information from professionals used to dealing with drug use unemotionally.
We recommend **www.talktofrank.com** and **www.connexions-direct.com**.

4 Sex and relationship problems

Underage sex

Over the last ten years, age at first sexual intercourse has dropped from 17 to 16 in the UK. Apart from the fact that under-16s are judged by the law to be too young, parents fear that their children are entering into sexual relationships too early and they may not take sufficient precautions against pregnancy and sexually transmitted infections (STIs).

It is very shocking for parents to discover that their under-16s are having sex. For many their immediate reaction is to get angry and want to lock up their children. But try to react in a calm way. Shouting, lecturing or bullying won't help. If your teen ever needs advice with a sexual or emotional matter in the future your behaviour at this stage will make it either more or less likely that they will come to you.

How old is your child and how big is the age gap between him/her and their partner? The younger the teen, the more likely it is that there is an exploitative element to the relationship, and the more concerned a parent should be. If you find out that your 13 to 14-year-old has had sex, especially if an older partner is involved, take action by talking to both of them. If the partner is much older they should be told not to contact your teen again.

With older teens, treat them as responsible young people and expect them to do the right thing. Make it clear what your views and expectations are, and emphasise that you expect and trust him/her to behave responsibly.

Make sure they are sensible enough to protect themselves again STIs and pregnancy.

Sexually transmitted infections

You can expect a young person who has contracted an STI to be ashamed, upset and even afraid. Although it's true that HIV and hepatitis infections can be fatal, most STIs can be cleared up quickly and simply with a course of antibiotics.

Medical help,can be found at:

☐ Genito-urinary medicine (GUM) clinics, available at most large hospitals
☐ Your GP
☐ Helplines:
NHS Direct 0845 46 47
NHS 24 (Scotland) 08454 24 24 24
fpa (formerly the Family Planning Association) 0845 310 1334
Sexual Health Line 0800 567 123
☐ Websites:
www.brook.org.uk
www.ruthinking.co.uk
www.malehealth.co.uk
www.tht.org.uk (Terrence Higgins Trust)

Chlamydia

One of the reasons that chlamydia is on the increase is that in the majority of cases there are no symptoms. When there are symptoms, they can include:

☐ Both sexes: discomfort during urination.
☐ Females: vaginal discharge, pelvic pain during sex, and bleeding between periods.
☐ Males: testicular pain and discharge from the penis.

Genital herpes

During its active phase, the herpes virus is very infectious. The first attack of herpes is usually the worst and subsequent attacks are usually less severe. Many people who get herpes don't have more attacks after the first one. Herpes is more likely to become active again at times when a person is run down or stressed. Symptoms include:

☐ Both sexes: tingling sensation about ten days after infection, followed by small watery blisters in the genital or anal areas. The blisters burst to leave painful sores, ulcers or crusts, and the sores take up to four weeks to heal. Sufferers may also experience a headache, temperature, swollen glands and aching muscles.

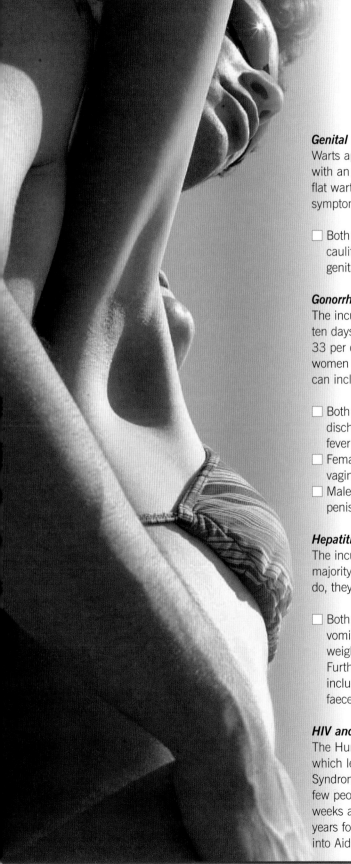

Genital warts or Human Papilloma Virus (HPV)

Warts appear one to three months after contact with an infected person. Although HPV can cause flat warts or an invisible infection, outward symptoms can include:

☐ Both sexes: one or several flat, hard or cauliflower-like lumps on the skin around the genital/anal area.

Gonorrhoea

The incubation period for gonorrhoea is two to ten days after having sex with an infected person. 33 per cent of men and over 50 per cent of women show no symptoms. Outward symptoms can include:

☐ Both sexes: painful urination, anal itching or discharge (after anal sex), and sore throat and fever (after oral sex).
☐ Females: yellowish or greenish, foul-smelling vaginal discharge.
☐ Males: yellowish or creamy discharge from the penis, testicular pain.

Hepatitis B and Hepatitis C

The incubation period is up to six months. In the majority of cases few symptoms occur. When they do, they include:

☐ Both sexes: flu-like symptoms, nausea, vomiting, tiredness, loss of appetite (and weight loss), muscle and joint aches. Further symptoms in the later stages may include jaundice, darker urine and paler faeces.

HIV and Aids

The Human Immuno-Deficiency Virus (HIV) which leads to Aids (Acquired Immune-Deficiency Syndrome) usually has no symptoms, although a few people experience flu-like symptoms about six weeks after exposure. It takes an average of nine years for an untreated HIV infection to develop into Aids.

LGV (Lymphomagranuloma Venereum)

LGV has been mainly confined to developing countries such as Africa, India and Asia until recently, when cases have been recorded in Europe and the UK. The incubation period is up to 30 days. Symptoms include:

☐ Both sexes: initially a small pimple in the genital region (which may not even be noticeable). Painful swelling in the groin area and/or open sores may develop as the infection spreads to the lymph nodes.

Pubic lice and scabies

Highly contagious, pubic lice and scabies are passed on by intimate physical contact. Although you can't catch them off a lavatory seat, scabies are not always picked up through sexual contact – holding hands with an infected person can be sufficient and they are sometimes rife in primary schools. Symptoms for both sexes include:

☐ Lice: louse droppings (like black dust) sometimes seen on underwear, itching in the infected area, and the lice themselves (which are just visible to the naked eye).

☐ Scabies: intense itching in affected areas and a rash where the scabies mites burrow into the skin.

Syphilis

The initial incubation period is up to six weeks. Symptoms for both sexes include:

☐ Primary stage: a painless ulcer wherever the syphilis bacteria got into the body (sometimes inside the anus or the vagina), which disappears of its own accord after a couple of weeks.

☐ Secondary stage: all-over infectious skin rash (especially on the palms and the soles of the feet), with brownish sores about the size of a 1p or 2p piece, sore throat, fever, headache, possibly wart-like growths on the genitals.

If untreated, the bacteria will become latent. If it becomes active later, the tertiary stage of syphilis – which can involve blindness, heart disease, joint damage, and mental illness – can be fatal.

Trichomonas

Males tend to be symptomless carriers. If symptoms do appear (between 3–21 days after infection for both sexes) they include:

☐ Females: frothy, yellowish-green vaginal discharge, and pain, itching and inflammation around the cervix, vagina, and vulva.

☐ Males: penile discharge and pain on urination.

See Chapter 5 for advice on how to avoid STIs in the future.

Abusive relationships

What can you do if you fear your teen has become involved in an abusive relationship? An abusive relationship can manifest itself in physical violence but can also involve psychological manipulation, pressure to commit deeply to a relationship that your teen is unsure about, or aggressive encouragement to join in a culture which endorses dangerous behaviour such as crime or drug-taking.

The relationship will probably be with a boyfriend or girlfriend but can also be with an abusive friend, when bullying goes beyond the playground. A key technique of a manipulator is to befriend someone before using them.

■ **Talk to your teen using the 'active listening' techniques described in Chapter 6**
The single biggest warning sign is if the partner you're worried about has been in a violent relationship before. Abusive individuals seldom change.

■ **Your teen may think 'It will be different with me – the other ones didn't deal with it properly'**
Your child may have an ideal of saving their friend or partner from themselves. Almost without exception, abusers claim that they were really the victim.

■ **Look out for other possible warning signs**
These may include putting your child's friends down and/or making it difficult for them to maintain their social circle, and an explosive temper over trivial things. Also look out for constant criticism of your teen's weight, hair, clothes, etc.

■ **Erratic behaviour**
If the individual concerned suffers from mood swings which are so erratic that your teenager is constantly trying to assess their partner/friend's mood and seems to only think in terms of their friends needs. If the friend exhibits signs of possessiveness and jealousy, or if your teen is being questioned about where they have been and who they were with, you are right to be concerned.

You can help by offering support and acknowledging that one of the abuser's tactics will be to attempt to turn your child against you. Maintain an open door at all times and do not hesitate to seek advice from a recognised support organisation.

5 Legal aspects

Criminal responsibility
☐ The law says that under-10s cannot be held responsible for a crime.
☐ Children aged 10 and above can be arrested, charged and taken to court in the same way as adults, but between the ages of 10–17 young people appear in the youth court.
☐ Between the ages of 10 and 14 a child can be convicted of a criminal offence if the prosecution can show that they were aware that what they were doing was seriously wrong.
☐ After the age of 14 the law considers teenagers fully responsible for their actions in the same way as an adult. In terms of criminal responsibility, they will be treated as an adult in a court of law (although not in terms of sentencing).

Age of Consent
☐ Over-16s in England, Scotland and Wales can legally consent to homosexual (gay) or heterosexual (straight) sex.
☐ Over-17s in Northern Ireland can legally consent to have sex.
☐ Under-18s cannot consent to have sex with someone in a 'position of trust' over them, such as youth carers, doctors or teachers.

The law sees underage sex, including consensual sex, as sexual assault, which is a criminal offence. A boy who has sex with a girl aged 13–15 could go to prison for two years, and sex with a girl under 13 carries a maximum sentence of life imprisonment. Girls aged 16 or over can be prosecuted for indecent assault if they have sex with a boy under 16. However, in reality consenting couples of around the same age are unlikely to be prosecuted.

Licensing Act 1964
☐ Under 14s are not allowed into a bar or pub unless the pub has a 'children's certificate'. Without this certificate, they can only go into parts that aren't licensed and where alcohol is either sold but not drunk (eg an off-sales area) OR drunk but not sold (eg a beer garden).
☐ 14 and 15-year-olds can go anywhere in a pub but cannot drink alcohol.
☐ 16 and 17-year-olds can buy or consume beer, cider or perry (plus wine in Scotland) with a meal, but only in a specified dining area (not at the bar).
☐ Unless they are having a pub meal, it's against the law for under-18s to buy alcohol in a pub, off-licence or supermarket. Buying alcohol for someone under 18 is also illegal.

Tattooing of Minors Act 1969
It is a criminal offence to tattoo anyone under the age of 18.

Misuse of Drugs Act 1971
It is an offence under this act to:
☐ Possess a controlled substance unlawfully.
☐ Possess a controlled substance with intent to supply it.
☐ Unlawfully supply a controlled drug (even where no charge is made for the drug).
☐ Allow premises you occupy or manage to be used for the purpose of drug-taking (eg you are technically breaking the law if you permit your teenager to smoke cannabis in their bedroom).

The Misuse of Drugs act classifies drugs (or 'controlled substances') into three different categories, known as Classes A, B and C. Class A drugs are those considered to be the most harmful, while drugs classified C are considered to be less dangerous.

Road Traffic Act 1972
It is an offence to drive while under the influence

of drink and/or drugs, including illegal and prescribed substances. Anyone found guilty of causing death by dangerous driving can face a lengthy prison sentence and an unlimited fine.

Children and Young Persons (Protection from Tobacco) Act 1991
It is illegal to sell tobacco products, including cigarettes, to people under the age of 16.

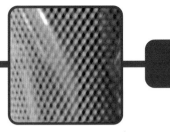

6 Other risky behaviour with long-term implications

Truancy

As a parent you have the legal responsibility for making sure your child attends school regularly until they reach school leaving age. If you are having problems:

☐ Talk to your child about the importance of attending school regularly and emphasise how important it is for them to be in class. Encourage them to see beyond the current term and look to their future hopes, which can only be fulfilled by gaining qualifications. State your expectations that they attend school. Look at your family's attitude and ask what messages are you giving? (do you allow your children to take time off to go on holidays abroad?).

☐ Take an active interest in your child's

schoolwork. Ask them about their day and praise and encourage their achievements at school.

☐ Talk to the teachers. If your child tells you they are bored at school or are having problems keeping up, ask to meet with the staff. They will be happy to talk to you.

☐ If your child makes excuses to try to avoid going to school, listen to them – you may find there is an underlying problem. It could be problems with schoolwork, or it could be bullying.

☐ Make sure that your child gets to school on time – can you offer a lift or walk to the school together? Arriving late can be disruptive for your child and the other children in the class.

☐ Contact your local education welfare officers (EWOs) or education social workers, who can provide professional help

Stealing

Stealing amongst younger children is serious, but in teenagers it can be a gateway to criminal behaviour. The motivation behind theft can involve a desire for attention, bravado, wish-fulfilment and fantasy, or even revenge.

Investigate your teenager's reasons for stealing. Are they taking things from fellow students or are they shoplifting? Are they being pressured into stealing because of bullying or is it a simple desire to 'have better stuff'?

Be very clear that you consider stealing to be wrong, regardless of the motive.

Petty theft, such as shoplifting, may be dealt with at home. Ask your teen if they understand the consequences if caught and if they realise that others may suffer for their actions.

Sometimes the first time a parent realises that their child is stealing is when they are contacted by a store detective or police officer. Usually the professional involved is very experienced in dealing with this sort of problem and can put you in touch with appropriate organisations to tackle it.

Often the seriousness of being caught and cautioned is enough to make a young person reconsider and change their behaviour.

Violence

Abusive language and respect

What if your teen becomes violent and abusive to other family members and their day to day behaviour is persistently unpleasant and unacceptable?

The first question to ask is 'What is the motivation behind these outbursts?' Are they a sign of some deeper anger or distress that you are unaware of or just a lack of self-control? In the former case when things are peaceful and everyone is getting on well, take the opportunity to talk to your son or daughter. It's a good idea to get away from the house by going out for a walk or to have a bite to eat together - that way you are unlikely to be distracted by household matters. Talk about how they are feeling. Now it becomes a matter of self control.

It's a common worry that by acknowledging a feeling you will add to it. Just the opposite is true. By acknowledging the feeling, especially if it is a 'bad' one like anger, resentment or jealousy, you are letting them know it's okay to have those feelings. Acknowledging the feeling isn't the same as condoning it.

You can't change the feeling, and you can't do anything about the way your child feels, but you can make it clear that it's not alright to act on such feelings.

If your son smacks his sister for breaking his video game, then you might say: 'I can see that you are angry with your sister for breaking your game' (feelings accepted) 'but it's not okay to hit her' (behaviour limited).

Occasionally, teenagers become abusive to their parents, especially when they are bigger. This is a form of domestic violence and sympathetic outside help should be sought without delay. Contact the National Domestic Violence Helpline (0808 200 0247, **www.refuge.org.uk**).

Self-harm

The majority of teenagers who self-harm do not intend their actions to be a suicide attempt. However, it is their means of coping with difficulties and emotional problems. Self-injury can be:

☐ A sign of emotional distress
☐ A sign of sexual, physical or emotional abuse
☐ A sign of being bullied
☐ A symptom of low self-esteem
☐ A reaction to rejection or neglect
☐ An expression of grief or anger

Many people who self-harm feel a 'high' afterwards, which comes from the sense of relief and the release of endorphins after the injury. Self-harming can become compulsive or addictive. A number of self-harmers report that they don't know their motivation for what they do.

Professional help is important for a teenager who is self-harming. They are usually deeply distressed and need understanding and support. A useful website is available at **www.selfharm.org.uk**.

7 What to do when your teen is a victim

Assaults, muggings, hate crimes, and sexual harassment don't only happen to adults. If the worst does happen to your teenager, go to the police as soon as possible. This is not always easy and young people can be understandably reluctant. As well as reporting a crime in person, it's possible to use the police's non-emergency website (**www.online.police.uk**) or call Crimestoppers anonymously on 0800 555 111.

In an emergency, call 999.

When a crime is reported, the police will ask if you'd like to be referred to Victim Support, which offers free advice about practical concerns such as compensation, insurance and police and court procedures. It can also provide someone to talk to in confidence and can put victims in touch with counsellors or other support organisations. Victim Support can be contacted on 0845 30 30 900 (or visit the website at **www.victimsupport.org.uk**) and is open to anyone who has been affected by crime.

Strong emotional reactions can follow after a crime takes place. Shock, withdrawal and fearfulness are common, but so are anger and a desire for revenge, or even guilt ('How could I be so stupid as to let that happen?'). In the longer term reactions can take the form of depression, or physical symptoms like headaches and insomnia.

The type of crime and the circumstances in which it happened affect how your teenager may cope. Being mugged by a stranger is very different from long-term harassment by someone you know. Support, encouragement and a listening ear are essential when recovering from a serious crime.

Chapter 9

Education, earning and independence

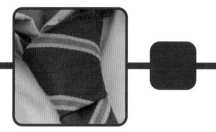

1 Choosing a secondary school

When deciding on which secondary school, think about who your child is and what their individual needs are, as well as the school's reputation. Don't rely on academic results alone, nor what other parents say. Keep an open mind. There are a variety of different schools designed to meet the special talents of different children – what's best for one won't necessarily suit another child, even if they are siblings.

☐ You can find out about your local schools online or directly from your local authority, who can send you a list of all the schools in your area. Individual schools usually have their own websites (often created by the pupils themselves) which can give a flavour of what the school is like. Ofsted Reports are available online at **www.ofsted.gov.uk/reports/**

☐ Talk to your child's primary school teachers. They know their academic capabilities and they know the local secondary schools, so they are well placed to advise on the type of school that would best suit your child.

☐ What type of school? Are you a member of a faith group and do you want your child to attend a faith school? When applying to a faith school, it is not necessary for the family to endorse the particular faith, or attend regular worship, but it counts for a lot.

☐ If you can afford it, you may want your child to go to an independent (fee-paying) school. Many of these schools have admission exams and 'feeder schools' which prepare pupils for the entrance exam. If your child is in a state school, extra tuition may be needed if they are to have a good chance of passing the exam. Parents are attracted to independent schools by their high standards of academic attainment, their ethos and the wide range of facilities available. For more info, visit the Independent Schools Council website at **www.isc.co.uk**

☐ Does your child have particular skills or talents? City Technology Schools are geared towards science, technology and the world of work, offering a range of vocational qualifications as well as GCSEs and A-levels. Some schools have specialist status; they focus on particular subject areas including sports, languages, technology or visual arts but must also meet the National Curriculum requirements and deliver a broad and balanced education to all pupils.

☐ Make a shortlist of suitable schools and visit them on open days. Informally, you can find out more information by asking other parents whose children are already at the schools on your shortlist.

☐ Even if you live in the catchment area, or your child is at a 'feeder' primary school, don't assume a place is automatic. Many schools set their own admission procedures and only those who apply via the standard application route are considered. Being close to the school is no guarantee of a place.

2 Education timeline

What happens when?
- Year 07 = 11 to 12-year-olds
- Year 08 = 12 to 13-year-olds
- Year 09 = 13 to 14-year-olds
- Year 10 = 14 to 15-year-olds
- Year 11 = 15 to 16-year-olds
- Year 12 = 16 to 17-year-olds
- Year 13 = 17 to 18-year-olds

Starting out

Most children start secondary school at the beginning of the September before their 12th birthday and begin Key Stage Three (KS3). KS3 usually lasts for three years, although a condensed two-year KS3 is being piloted in some schools.

The Department for Education and Skills sets official 'targets for every child' in each subject, describing what children should be able to do and know.

- ☐ To find out more about what your child is learning at each stage of secondary school, visit the DfES website at **www.dfes.gov.uk**.
- ☐ For more general help and advice, visit the Parent Centre section of the DfES website at **www.parentscentre.org.uk**.
- ☐ For the latest information about the National Curriculum, go to **www.nc.uk.net**.

It is assumed when children enter secondary school that they have mastered the 'Three Rs', although a significant percentage of children will still need help with basic skills. In secondary school, emphasis moves to increasing specialisation, in either sciences, languages, or

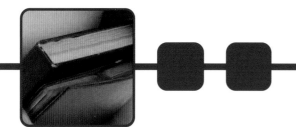

the humanities. During this period, most parents will find that they are progressively less able to help their children with their homework.

If they are to succeed in mastering the secondary school curriculum and achieve their full potential, teenagers will have to develop good organisational skills and study habits.

Homework

Throughout the first five years of secondary school, suggested homework time increases from 20–30 minutes per subject in Year 7, to about five hours per subject per week in Year 11. To an extent, homework time commitments vary between subjects that demand a lot of reading and writing, such as English or History, and practical subjects, such as sport or drama.

How to help your teen develop good study habits

☐ Work with, rather than against, the body clock. Some young people prefer to get down to homework as soon as they come home from school; others prefer some chill-out time before they feel ready to concentrate again. Whichever they prefer, a regular evening homework slot is the best thing. In this way they are unlikely to keep putting it off until the last minute.

☐ Make sure they have a good place to study undisturbed. Whatever they say, no-one can study effectively lying on the floor in front of the television. A good environment for study should have the following:
  ◆ A quiet place where they are not disturbed. If the room in which they study is shared with a sibling, schedule homework before the sibling has to go to bed. Discourage siblings from going in and out of the room when your teen is doing their homework. (This also sends a message to the younger child that homework is important.)
  ◆ Good light and temperature with chair and desk at the correct height
  ◆ A suitable desk or work surface, large

enough for reference books, note books and possibly a PC.
  ◆ Storage space for reference books and files, pens and paper, art materials etc.

☐ Cut out virtual distractions. When homework is done on a PC, there is greater likelihood of being distracted; MSN messages, incoming emails and pop-up reminders undermine concentration. Explain to your son or daughter that in anything we do, getting started is the most difficult thing. Once they have 'got into' what they are doing, it becomes increasingly easy. If they are constantly distracted, they are always starting again and never get 'on a roll'. Their work will suffer as a result.

☐ As a parent, send out a clear message that homework is top priority by showing an interest. If you have a copy of their lesson timetable and exam timetable, it's much easier to talk about what's going on at school. If they are finding something difficult, encourage them to explain it to you. This can help them get their thoughts straight.

☐ Sometimes it's tempting to do the work for them, especially when the topic is something you are interested in. By all means, discuss the assignment together. However, doing the work for them will have negative long-term effects. You'll be learning a lot, but they won't!

☐ The internet is widely used and can be a fantastic resource but needs to be used wisely and not copied wholesale. Websites are not always reliable, so encourage your teenagers to discriminate when researching online and to check the sources for any results found. Numerous sites exist where students can download essays on almost any topic. Potential plagiarists should be aware that teachers and examiners know about these sites too, and have methods of screening coursework for copied work. Cheating may jeopardise a student's whole school career.

☐ As homework gets more time consuming, many teenagers will lose motivation and concentration.

Parents can play an important role in encouraging their teenager to keep focussed. Take an interest in what they are doing. Ask regularly how they are getting on in various subjects and, when you know they have completed a piece of work, ask what mark they got and what feedback the teacher gave.

☐ Keep the goal of succeeding to the best of their ability to the front of their minds. Remind them that sound academic qualifications mean a good job, a university or higher education qualification. Explain that once students 'get into' subjects, they often find them really interesting. Don't nag or lecture but make it clear that you expect them to do their best and that means working hard and consistently.

☐ Bearing this in mind, some helpful sites include:
♦ BBC GCSE revision guide:
  www.bbc.co.uk/schools/gcsebitesize
♦ BBC AS Guru:
  www.bbc.co.uk/education/asguru
♦ BBC Scottish Standard Grade revision guide:
  www.bbc.co.uk/scotland/education/bitesize
♦ BBC Scottish Highers revision guide:
  **www.bbc.co.uk/scotland/education/
  bitesize/higher**
♦ Comprehensive resources for older students
  (part of the Guardian newspaper website)
  www.learnthings.co.uk
♦ Wikipedia
  www.wikipedia.org
  A great reference site, if used within reason!
  Beware of unsubstantiated claims – most
  reputable entries have a long list of sources,
  which can then be used to verify information.

Note: At the time of writing, education in the UK is prone to change and variation. If you or your teenager is confused, the best people to ask for advice are their teachers. They will be familiar with the latest developments and options, and can help navigate through the system. If you are wondering what NVQ, UCAS, PSHE or any of the other abbreviations that litter the educational world mean, consult the panel on page 147.

3 Years 07–13: key points and activities

Year 07 (11–12 years)
The first year in secondary school can be a difficult one for students. They have to deal with being little fishes in a big pool, and a more complicated curriculum with many different subjects and different teachers. At the same time they are entering puberty, with all the emotional turmoil that goes with it. Not all pupils settle down well. Younger kids may also be susceptible to bullying in a big school and parents should be on the look-out for signs that their son or daughter is not adjusting to their new environment. If by the second term your son or daughter hasn't settled in and you suspect a problem, the Head of Year takes overall responsibility for pupils' pastoral development. Form tutors will usually deal with day-to-day issues.

Pupils are required to do about 20–30 minutes homework per subject (usually three) per night. Most schools provide pupils with a 'journal' or contact book to log timetables, homework tasks and reminders. It's also the key link between parents and teachers. School policy may encourage you to write notes in the journal in order to explain absence, illness, reasons for lateness, no PE kit and so on.

Year 08 (12–13years)
This is the last year before exam pressures begin in earnest. Most children will have settled into a routine by now and will have made friends. Many children thoroughly enjoy Year 08. Pupils who did well in Year 07 may be moved up into a different 'band' or 'set'. This may cause initial disruption and be unsettling, but it can also be a good motivator.

Year 08 also sees the start of the Action Project, which focusses on pupils with behavioural difficulties and tries to address and support them.

The recommended amount of homework for Year 08 is three subjects per night with 30–40 minutes spent on each. Exams tend to be timetabled towards the end of the school year.

Expect a report for each subject. A Parents' Evening is usually organised around this time.

Year 09 (13–14 years)
At the beginning of May, Year 09 pupils take the SATs. Standard Assessment Tests – or SATs – are the first set of formal public exams in secondary school.

There are eight levels of attainment, each corresponding to certain pre-determined standards, so you can see how your child is progressing relative to the expected standard for their age.

By the end of January, expectations and demands are more focussed and individualised. Teachers will often work through mock SAT papers with pupils to familiarise them with the layout and format of the paper before the summer exams. Pupils' abilities in English, Maths, Science, History, Geography, Modern Foreign Languages, Design & Technology, Information Technology, Art, Music, Physical Education and Citizenship are also assessed.

Taking into account their test and assessment results, previous academic performance, and their personal likes and dislikes, your teenager will discuss and decide on which Key Stage Four (KS4) qualifications to aim for. This is the stage at which most pupils will choose the range of GCSE subjects (or the equivalent) they are going to sit.

Schools may also offer the option of Entry Level Certificates for pupils who would find GCSEs difficult.

Homework is ratchetting up now and pupils are set homework in three subjects per night, taking around 45 minutes over each. There will also be exams in non-SAT subjects. Parents will receive a report and an invitation to a 'progress evening' at the end of the year.

Year 10 (14–15 years)
KS4 begins and pupils start their GCSE coursework and/or begin working towards other qualifications. This is an important year for the

whole GCSE course. The bulk of the syllabus for each subject is taught in Year 10 and revised and revisited in Year 11. The homework load should be 45–60 minutes on each of three subjects per evening.

■ Work experience

During Year 10 pupils are encouraged to think about their work experience placement. This usually lasts for two weeks and gives pupils the opportunity to work in their chosen area of interest. It can often act as a motivator, providing pupils with direction whilst making them more aware of the demands of working.

Year 11 (15–16 years)

Most schools have mock GCSEs around Christmas and the GCSE exams themselves normally start in May. Your teenager may be given study leave before the exams, in order to revise away from school.

Courses for entry level certificates and NVQs are usually completed by the end of Year 11.

This is the last year of compulsory education, so it's also time to plan post-16 options – AS and A-level, International Baccalaureate, BTECs, OCR Nationals, NVQs, Key Skills Level 3, GCEs in applied subjects. All of these can be taken at Level 3 on the NQF, which is the same Level as

A-levels, and are awarded points on the UCAS (Universities & Colleges Admissions Service) tariff.

If a teenager opts to start work, it doesn't mean that learning ceases. Parents of working teenagers should encourage them to get further training to improve their employability.

☐ Modern Apprenticeships combine on-the-job training with classroom learning.

☐ The 'Time Off for Study or Training' programme means a young person is legally entitled to study towards a qualification during normal working hours and still get paid.

☐ Also available for 16 to 18-year-olds is 'Entry to Employment' (e2e) which is intended to help young people progress towards an apprenticeship, further learning or a job. It covers learning in three core areas: vocational development, basic and key skills, and personal and social development.

Date for your diary: GCSE exam results are announced on the last Thursday in August. Scottish Standard and Higher Grade exam results come out on the same day, usually the second Tuesday of August.

Year 12 (16–17 years)

This is the year when Advanced Subsidiary (AS) Level exam courses are taken. An AS-level represents the first half of the full A-level and is worth 50 per cent of the marks.

Many pupils aren't just beginning new courses but starting at a new school or college too. Sixth form college is usually less structured than school and, although it is a good opportunity for students to learn to organise themselves, it can be difficult to make the transition. AS-levels are much more demanding than GCSEs and there is more independent study, less spoon-feeding.

Most AS-level courses are modular and the first set of exams fall at the end of the first term or beginning of the second, so it's important to get off to a good start and not fall behind. During the first term students should meet with the form tutor (or whoever has responsibility for pastoral care) to discuss progress.

Date for your diary: AS-Level results are announced on the third Thursday in August.

Year 13 (17–18 years)

A-level students confirm which AS-Level subjects they will continue to study and convert to A-levels. Most choose two or three subjects. Since 2002, schools may offer the option of Advanced Extension Awards (AEAs), designed to stretch the most able students.

As well as exams, your teenager will also be expected to present their National Curriculum 'Key Skills' portfolio – usually a file or folder of evidence showing they have achieved competency in various areas.

For pupils planning to apply to university, Universities & Colleges Admissions Service (UCAS) entries are submitted in December for a mid-January deadline. However, for candidates to Oxford or Cambridge, and medical or veterinary schools, the closing date is mid-October. For especially competitive courses, some universities are now setting additional tests, such as the Bio-Medical Admissions Test (BMAT) or the National Admissions Test for Law (LNAT) to assist with the selection of candidates.

Date for your diary: A-level results are announced on the third Thursday in August. Scottish Higher results are usually published on the second Tuesday in August.

Post-18 education

There are plenty of higher education choices available, including university degrees, sandwich courses, foundation degrees, Higher National Diploma/Higher National Certificate (HND/HNC) and DipHE.

Some teenagers prefer to go straight into full-time employment once they have gained their A-level qualifications – it's still possible to gain further qualifications while holding down a job.

4 Which subjects?

At 14 or 15 years old

Choosing what to study at KS4 (14–15 years) is probably the first big decision of your teenager's life. It can have far-reaching implications, especially if they drop a subject which is required for future career choices – for example, English, Maths and Science are compulsory at GCSE, but an aspiring fashion stylist won't get very far without additional qualifications in art and design.

Before making their subject choices, teenagers should have the chance to discuss their options fully with someone who knows their academic strengths and weaknesses. Young people have a variety of professionals they can talk to, including Connexions advisors (**www.connexions-direct.com**), careers advisors, careers teachers and form tutors.

Parents will want to talk the choices through with their teens before they make their final decision. Listen to them too. Be wary of steering them in a direction you think will suit them, or of encouraging them to go for subjects you enjoyed – their talents and dreams may be very different.

Some subjects, – English, maths, information and communication technology (ICT) and science – are compulsory. For the remainder students make their own choices.

Most schools stipulate that pupils make choices within certain bands of subjects, so their final choices should ideally include at least one subject from mathematics, languages, sciences, technology and the arts. KS4 options should aim to be balanced, but students should also think about what they enjoy. They are much more likely to work hard to gain a qualification in a subject they like than one they think they 'ought' to do.

At 16 or 17 years old:

Teenagers tend to make Level Three Qualifications (16–17 years) choices based on their aptitude for a subject, combined with how much they enjoy it and, importantly, the impact their choice will have on their further studies and career. These may seem daunting decisions to make at the age of 16 but, important as they are, it is unlikely they are closing off other options forever. Many universities now offer modular degrees with a wide ranging mix of subjects. Career changes are much more common in the 21st century and there is still room for flexibility after Level Three Qualifications – and beyond! Although a would-be doctor would be ill-advised to study only English, Art and History at A level, several universities now have special 'Access to Medicine' courses allowing arts graduates to retrain as medics if they change their minds later on.

5 A rough guide to qualifications

The changes in secondary school education over the past 20 years have been significant and the new range of targets and qualifications baffling. Some of the significant changes introduced in the last generation include:

National Qualifications Framework

There are lots of qualifications available to young people in the UK, but for a qualification to be recognised nationally it has to be part of the National Qualifications Framework (NQF).

There are three categories and nine levels of qualification within the NQF, from Entry Level up to Level 8. You can find out more about the wide range of potential qualifications from the Qualifications and Curriculum Authority website: **www.qca.org.uk**

The qualifications most commonly studied for are:

■ GCSE

GCSEs replaced O-levels and CSEs in 1988. Instead of a single exam, GCSE students are assessed on a combination of exams and coursework over an extended period, which count towards the final grade.

Coursework is research or projects that can include essays, fieldwork reports, artwork, making products or investigations, and is often worked on at home, in the student's own time. While parents are welcome to provide support and encouragement, it's important to resist the temptation to get carried away and do the coursework for your teenager. Penalties for cheating are severe.

Guidelines from the Qualifications & Curriculum Authority (QCA) are very explicit about what is, and is not, allowed:
A parent or teacher must not put pen to paper –

Abbreviations

ACCAC:	The Qualifications, Curriculum and Assessment Authority for Wales – Awdurod Cymwsterau, Cwricwlwm Ac Asesu Cymru.
AEA:	Advanced Extension Award.
AEN:	Additional Educational Needs.
A-level:	Advanced level. The A-level is the six-unit GCE. It consists of the AS and a further three units called the A2.
AS-level:	Advanced Subsidiary level.
BMAT:	Bio-Medical Admissions Test.
BTEC:	Qualifications awarded by the British Training and Enterprise Council.
CATs:	Cognitive Ability Tests.
CCEA:	Council for the Curriculum, Examinations and Assessment for Northern Ireland.
CSE:	Certificate of Secondary Education.
DfES:	Department for Education and Skills.
e2e:	Entry to Employment.
EMA:	Education Maintenance Allowance.
G&T:	'Gifted and Talented' (not gin and tonic!).
GCE:	General Certificate of Education.
GCSE:	General Certificate for Secondary Education.
GNVQ:	General National Vocational Qualification.
HE:	Higher Education.
HND:	Higher National Diploma.
IB:	International Baccalaureate – an internationally-recognised alternative to A-levels.
KS3:	Key Stage Three.
LNAT:	National Admissions Test for Law.
MidYIS:	Middle Years Information System.
NC:	National Curriculum.
NQF:	National Qualifications Framework.
NVQ:	National Vocational Qualification.
OCR:	Oxford, Cambridge and the Royal Society of Arts Examinations Board.
O-level:	Ordinary level.
PSHE:	Personal, Social & Health Education.
QCA:	Qualifications and Curriculum Authority for England.
UCAS:	Universities and Colleges Admissions Service.
VCE:	Vocational Certificate of Education.

students must write the coursework themselves. A parent or teacher can discuss the project with the student, but they must not give direct advice on what the student should or should not write. Students are given classroom tests and assessed as they progress through the GCSE syllabus. Coursework means there is less chance of an unanticipated poor grade.

GCSEs are graded from A* to G in each subject, followed by 'U', which means 'ungraded'. A grade of D or below, in a potential A-level subject, calls for serious thought about whether to sit the GCSE again in the expectation of a better grade, or to reconsider A-level subject options. However, a GCSE grade of D or below as a Level 1 qualification on the NQF may well help the student to then go on and study that or other subjects at Level 2.

■ AS-level

AS-levels can act as a foundation for A-levels or as a qualification in their own right. They were designed so students can mix and match AS and A-levels with vocational A-levels and other qualifications to suit their individual needs.

AS-levels are made up of three units, which can count towards the six units required for a full A-level. They are assessed on coursework and end-of-course exams.

Unlike the old A-level system, which ended in 2000, the frequency of important deadlines can make the AS-level year a stressful one for teenagers. The school will encourage them to work more independently than they did for GCSEs and it can take time for them to adjust. Support at home, and a quiet place to study, is important.

■ A-level

The A-level is the six-unit GCE. It consists of the AS and a further three units called the A2. In Year 13, students can choose to specialise in three or four of their AS subjects at A-level. The AS-level work will count towards the final A-level mark and the coursework/exam assessment format is the same.

6 University

University applications are made through UCAS, which is the UK central organisation that processes entries to higher education. Applications are made online (**www.ucas.co.uk**). Students without internet access at home complete their application forms at school.

Which University?

Students have a maximum of six choices of university. Deciding what and where to study is the first step. Things to consider include:

- [ ] Finance: money should be top of the list of considerations. University is a financial drain for both students and parents. Research shows that financial implications are the most worrying of issues for prospective students by far and have a big impact on choosing where to study. With the introduction of variable fees, not all universities charge the same. Apart from student loans, which are available to all UK students, students from poorer backgrounds may be eligible for additional means tested help. There are also various schemes to help students finance their education, such as scholarships, bursaries and loans, so research options on university websites and with your local LEA.
- [ ] What subject? Get hold of the prospectuses and read the outlines of all the different courses. Universities apparently offering the same subject may have completely different modules *eg* some English courses include an Old Norse option, others concentrate on 20th century American fiction.
- [ ] What final qualification does your teenager have in mind, and which institutions offer these qualifications? For example, students wishing to gain a degree in 'Surfing and Beach Management' will need to apply to the University of Wales, as this is currently the only institution offering this course.
- [ ] Living costs and the assistance a young person can receive varies, depending on where they study and whether or not they live at home. It's also worth investigating the graduate employment statistics for a university, to see how employable a graduate is going to be once they've got that expensive degree.
- [ ] What kind of environment does your teenager want to spend the next three years living in? Are they content to be based on an out-of-town campus, or will they be happier in the heart of a city?
- [ ] Will they go away to university or stay at home? One student in four now lives at home – it is worth considering if money is tight.
- [ ] Is geography a consideration? How often will they want to come home? Long-distance travel in term time is expensive.

Visiting is the best way to get a realistic feel for potential post-18 choices. Look at where students actually live, rather than the touristy areas. Some universities (such as York and Sussex) are located outside the city, while others (such as London) have very high rents and travel costs.

All universities now have their own websites, from which potential undergraduates can order a prospectus or get more information. The internet also offers more opportunities to find out unofficial opinions about courses and institutions (from current students or graduates) than was once the case!

The UCAS website (**www.ucas.co.uk**) is the most up-to-date source of information for university applicants. Procedures are changing rapidly (at the moment there is a movement to make university applications post-qualification by 2012) so it's very important to check up online and ensure that you've got the right information and exact dates.

Application timetable

- [ ] Start of September: application processing begins.
- [ ] Mid-October: deadline for Oxbridge and medicine, dentistry, veterinary science or veterinary medicine applications.

- Mid-January: closing date for applications from UK and EU students.
- Mid-March: applicants can refer themselves through Extra, which is a way of applying to further universities or colleges if any choices have been declined.
- End of March: application decisions should have arrived from universities and colleges.
- End of June: last date for receipt of applications for immediate consideration (those received after this date held for Clearing).
- Beginning of July: last date for applicants to refer themselves through Extra.
- Third Thursday in August: publication of GCE and VCE results and the start of vacancy information service.
- Five weeks after results: last date for receipt of applications (eg 20 September is the cut-off point if results are published on 16 August).

The application process

The success of an application depends on academic achievement to date, on information and estimated grades provided by the school or Sixth Form college, and the teenager's Personal Statement. This Personal Statement is the only opportunity a student has to personalise their university application and make it stand out. It should be their own work. Feedback is important, so encourage them to show first drafts to teachers, family members and other adults who may be able to help – eg family friends who have been to the same university or who have chosen a similar career to the one your teenager hopes to embark upon. Under no circumstances download a 'personal' statement from the internet. Many other students will have done the same. Admissions tutors are wise to this and will take a dim view. Stress to your prospective student that this is their one chance to make an impression, and they should invest time and effort in it.

Once the submission has been made, UCAS will send a 'welcome letter' (also known as an AS2 letter), including an individual application number, to say that the application has been processed. They will also be sent a password enabling them to use Track, an online application system that allows them to log in and see if any colleges or universities have decided to make them an offer.

Very few universities interview candidates these days. Given the rise in the number of applicants they just don't have time – it's only the 'selective' universities that tend to interview (and then not for all courses or all students). Most universities will make an offer based on a young person's existing and predicted grades, their academic references and their personal statement – so a lot rides on the application form, which should be thoroughly checked for spelling errors, grammar and punctuation.

If an interview is required, the format varies from place to place. If at all possible your teenager should try to organise a 'mock interview' at school or college, or with another knowledgeable adult. Knowing what to expect from an interview will help settle the interviewee's nerves.

If a young person has got the right grades when the results come out in August, and if they meet all the other conditions of their offer, the university's admissions tutor will confirm their place. If they get much better A-level results than expected, students can opt to re-apply to different universities (with higher entry qualifications) the following autumn.

If exam results are disappointing, first contact the university to see if the place could still be confirmed – this is not unusual, especially if there is only a narrow margin of failure. If not, the student is eligible for Clearing (this is also the case if they decline all offers). UCAS will send a Clearing Passport automatically. If students go through Clearing, they should be able to gain support and advice from their school or college to help them through the maze of places. Re-sits are also an option in the case of disappointing results.

Many students starting university are unsure about the precise nature of the course they have signed up for. They may make a wrong choice. These choices are not irreversible. If they don't like the course, remind your teen that university staff are always available to discuss issues like this and that it is always possible to change.

7 Life skills

Earning and managing money

By the time a young person leaves home they need to have some understanding of how to manage money, how to budget and how to avoid easy credit. Students inevitably incur debt while getting their degree; the trick is to keep it at a minimum.

Teenagers need to learn about budgeting long before they start earning and managing their own money. Children usually get some form of pocket money from an early age. In 2006, the UK average weekly pocket money for 12 to 16-year-olds was £9.76.

Talking about money is important, so include your teenager when you discuss family finances. You don't have to go into details – just explain that your budget isn't elastic and that you work hard for the money you earn. Discuss the comparative costs of everyday grocery items as well as luxuries. Talk about the things you or your teen could buy with the extra money.

Don't be ashamed to say you (or the family as a whole) can't afford something. It's the grown-up thing to do and your teen will learn by your example. Saying 'we can't afford it' rather than 'you can't have it' will often result in sympathy and practical attempts to improve the situation, rather than sulking.

■ Is an allowance a good idea?

Earning pocket money by doing chores can help young people appreciate how much time and effort it takes to earn enough for treats. At around 15–16 years, if you can afford it, think about giving an allowance. This does away with any feeling you may have that you are always doling out money to your teen. Many teens don't like asking for money and would prefer to be in charge of their own finances. Start by asking them to prepare a budget, so that you can decide together what a reasonable amount for clothes, music, magazines and entertainment would be (your opinions may differ). Don't forget to include out-of-the-ordinary expenses like

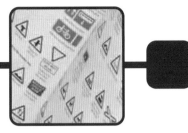

birthday presents or haircuts. Then let them decide how to spend it (a cashbook to keep track of costs is a good idea). If they blow the budget in the first month, tough! Being unable to buy the things they want for a few weeks or months will demonstrate the importance of careful budgeting far better than any lecture ever could.

Allow them to make their own financial mistakes, and don't bail them out – if they want to spend all of their pocket money on computer games, they will soon realise it's at the expense of being able to buy new clothes. Next time they will handle their budget better.

If they rack up extortionate mobile phone or internet bills, you will have to pay them yourself (under-18s cannot enter into a legal contract). However, agree that they will pay you back by an arranged date, either out of their allowance or out of extra cash earned by doing jobs around the house.

■ Credit

Credit cards and store cards are a dangerous temptation. It's inevitable your teenager will be deluged by offers of credit. Some smart and well-disciplined operators can turn the short-term zero per cent interest offer to their advantage, but unless your teenager is unusually mature and self-controlled, best advice is to avoid credit cards at all costs.

Once your teenager turns 18 it's worth considering putting one of your own household utilities bills into their name. Many gas, water, electrical and telecommunications companies require proof of a previous account with a utilities supplier, before they will allow a new applicant to open an account with them. A good 'credit history' at the family home can prove helpful once your teenager moves out of halls of residence and has to grapple with the practicalities of setting up their own household accounts in rented accommodation. (You will not be held responsible for bills at a different address).

■ Part-time working

Younger teenagers often earn extra money by doing chores, but as they get older taking on a part-time job is a good way of earning extra pocket money or saving for university or a car.

Children can begin paid work at 13, subject to certain regulations. During term time children may work a maximum of 12 hours per week – two hours maximum on school days and Sundays and a maximum of five hours on Saturdays for 13 to 14-year-olds; 15 to 16-year-olds are allowed to work up to eight hours on Saturdays during term time.

The rules are relaxed a little during school holidays, when 13 to 14-year-olds can work a maximum of 25 hours per week (five hours maximum on weekdays and Saturdays, and two hours maximum on Sundays), and 15 to 16-year-olds may work a maximum of 35 hours per week (eight hours maximum on weekdays and Saturdays, and two hours maximum on Sundays).

There are various other stipulations for employing people below school leaving age, including a ban on them working in pubs or betting shops, and on working for more than one hour before school.

The UK National Minimum Wage does not apply to under-18s, while 18 to 21-year-olds are paid a lower minimum than older workers, known as the Development Rate.

Taking paid employment for spending money can have more benefits for teenagers than simply having more money. They will have to take responsibility for turning up on time and doing tasks properly (even when they are boring), plus the workplace gives them the opportunity to talk to adults who have had different experiences from those of family and friends. Working can improve a teen's social skills, as well as provide the chance to practice mental arithmetic and written communication, and perhaps even to learn more esoteric skills such as silver service waiting or window-dressing.

Striking the right balance between studying and earning is important. If possible, taking a part-time job in a study-related field is a good compromise, as your teenager will be learning while they are earning, and creating potential contacts and referees for later life.

■ Learning to drive (and paying for it)

Driving is a useful skill, but learning to drive can be very expensive. Lessons cost around £25 per hour and the driving tests are £48.50 (practical) and £21.50 (theory). Most would-be drivers can expect to spend at least £300.

Things to consider before starting driving lessons are:

- [ ] Why learn to drive right now? There's a trend for people to wait until their early 20s before taking driving lessons. However, a full, clean driving licence can be an advantage when making job applications, so weigh up the pros and cons.
- [ ] How often will the chance to drive arise in the next few years? Ongoing driving practice is vital and if the young person is unlikely to drive much after passing the test, it might be wiser to wait.
- [ ] Can they afford to buy and maintain a car, insure it, and keep it fuelled?
- [ ] Do they have the time and opportunity to prepare for the tests? The Driving Standards Agency (DSA) recommends 45 hours' driving experience before taking the practical test. Are friends and family able and willing to take your teenager out for practice drives in their own vehicle?

Before learning to drive, your teenager needs a provisional driving licence (apply online or visit your local post office to obtain the D1 form), which cannot be issued to under-17s. Driving lessons are available

from large, national institutions such as the British School of Motoring, or from smaller companies and individuals. Ensure your teen is learning with a DSA Approved Driving Instructor (ADI).

Once they've passed their test, teenagers can take a Pass Plus course which teaches them things you only used to be able to pick up through experience, like driving at night, on motorways and in bad weather. As an added bonus, a Pass Plus qualification could make the difference of a year's driving experience to the cost of their insurance premium.

For young drivers, obtaining car insurance has often been a frustrating experience due to the sky-high premiums. It is a fact that younger drivers generally make more claims than their older counterparts, in part due to their lack of experience, and as such many insurance companies seem to price them out of the market.

However, more and more insurance companies are attempting to offer advantages to young, safe drivers. For example, some UK motor insurance companies have introduced a rapid bonus scheme, which runs for nine months rather than twelve, so the year's no-claims bonus is obtained more quickly and the next year's premium reduces more quickly as a result.

Other companies offer young driver insurance, which provide flexible payment options and cover for provisional licence holders.

■ Eating properly

Teens are used to being catered for at home where someone else is responsible for buying, preparing and serving the food they eat. Now they're moving out, they have to feed themselves. A young person who leaves home without being able to boil an egg won't get very far.

Make sure they have some basic skills before they go. Discuss what comprises a balanced diet and encourage your adolescent to practice shopping and cooking at home by preparing a family meal once a week. On a limited budget, young people need to know how to shop for bargains. Comparing prices, finding special offers, getting value packs and end-of-the-day discounts all make a substantial saving on the week's food bill.

Anyone can learn to make simple standby dishes like spaghetti bolognaise or vegetable chilli. There are good starter cookbooks available which assume nothing – we can recommend *How To Cook* by Delia Smith (a series of three books aimed at beginners, covering all the basics); *Grub on a Grant* by Cas Clarke (the old favourite – Cas Clark has now brought out *More Grub on Less Grant* for 21st-century students); *Real Fast Food* by Nigel Slater (simple, quick recipes with the emphasis on fresh ingredients; good for showing how to make high-quality dishes that cost less than ready meals); and *Cooking Up A Storm – The Teen Survival Cookbook* by Sam Stern (15-year-old foodie Sam shares 120 easy-to-cook recipes aimed squarely at the teen market).

■ Keeping house

Teenagers may complain bitterly about helping with chores, but getting to grips with the basics at home is important before being let loose in their own space.

Decide your own basic household rules (hopefully these will become ingrained long before your offspring leave home), such as:

☐ No food left out to attract mice, cockroaches or other unwanted visitors.
☐ No lamps left on, which waste electricity and may cause a fire if knocked over.
☐ Keeping 'public' spaces (eg the kitchen and bathroom) clean.

☐ Checking doors and windows are locked before going out.
☐ Don't leave valuables (especially laptops) in full view of windows.

When they go away to university, many students assume their possessions are still covered by their parents' household insurance. This may not automatically follow and items such as bicycles may have to itemised on your policy.

Their rooms may not be up to your standards of cleanliness, but as long as they are not a danger to health and safety, don't get into a fight about it.

When they are old enough to follow the instructions on the machine, they are old enough to wash their own clothes. Get them acquainted with the washing machine, making sure they know about removing coins and tissues from pockets and separating colours.

Simple safety rules should become second nature: don't dry clothes in front of gas fires; don't leave candles and joss sticks burning unattended; fit a smoke alarm and so on

■ Is your teen ready to leave home?

A desire for independence is not a personal rejection of their parents, but rather a natural part of a young person's move towards adulthood.

Most young people are excited about the possibility of moving away from home and living independently, but a few are anxious about it. Preparation is the best way to deal with nervousness. Look objectively at your teenager's maturity level and survival skills:

☐ Can they take care of themselves? Do they know how to cook, do laundry, eat well etc?
☐ Can they manage a budget?
☐ Are they able to make friends? Many Universities operate a 'buddy system' to help new students settle in and meet one another.
☐ Will they be able to organise their academic work?

Show confidence in their ability to meet new challenges. Provide practical help where necessary. Remind them that whether they need advice, or just want to talk over a problem, you are always just a phone call away.

The move to a university or job in a new town is an opportunity for a teen to finally 'try out' independent life, without having to leave the family for good. Sometimes a down-period comes a few weeks into the university term, when all the excitement of the introductory weeks has passed and the reality of life away from family and old friends sinks in. This is probably a good time for a visit.

Regular phone calls will help to reassure you that they are managing successfully. Your teen may also find this a comforting link with home and a good opportunity to ask for advice. Don't forget 'care packages' sent from home! Tuck in notes from family and friends along with favourite snacks and other treats.

8 Empty nest

Having sent the kids on their way with good qualifications and able to cook, clean and look after themselves, parents can congratulate themselves on a job well done. Now parents have more time to themselves and a tidier and quieter house. But while your son or daughter is adjusting to a new life away from you, you will also be adjusting to a new kind of life – one without at least one of your children. Your nest may not be totally empty, but at least one of the chicks has flown.

At this point many parents feel rather low and bereft. After all, you have devoted 18 years to raising your child, so now that they no longer need your day-to-day care and are no longer around the house feelings of loss and sadness are hardly surprising. It's not unusual for mothers to have an occasional weep. These feelings are perfectly natural. If, on the other hand, you feel that your useful life has ended, or if you are crying excessively, you should consult your doctor.

Finally . . .

☐ Don't get emotional with your teen. Be sensitive to the fact that at this stage your son or daughter will be dealing with their own issues.

☐ Keep in touch regularly, but give your teenager some space and don't feel rejected if they are not always able to take your calls. Buy some credit for your son's or daughter's mobile phone and agree a time you can have a long chat together.

☐ Take all the help and support you can get from your friends. Maybe some of them are going through the same thing, or have gone through it.

☐ Treat yourself. You may have lost a teenager, but you have gained a bathroom, so enjoy the luxury of a long relaxing bath.

You have been a parent for a long time, but now you need to think about your own future as a unique and individual human being. You hopefully have a lot more of your life yet to live, so get back in touch with who you are – build up your confidence and start planning to really make something of your new-found freedom!

Useful contacts

GENERAL HELP

Parentline Plus
www.parentlineplus.org.uk
A national charity providing information and support to parents and their families. Runs a national freephone help line (0808 800 2222) and Parent Network courses for parents. The majority of calls to its helpline are from the parents of teenagers.

Raisingkids.co.uk
www.Raisingkids.co.uk
Comprehensive website for parents of children of all ages. Good section on teenagers plus the opportunity to talk to other parents of teens and share experiences. Expert opinion on teens available from experienced Youth Worker.

DfES Parents' Centre
www.parentscentre.gov.uk
A section of the Department for Education and Skills' website aimed specifically at parents offering information and advice about education, the curriculum and finding a school.

Families Need Fathers
www.fnf.org.uk
FNF is a registered charity, principally concerned with the problems of maintaining a child's relationship with both parents during and after family breakdown. FNF provides information and support to parents of either sex.

PinkParents UK
www.pinkparents.org.uk
Offers information, advice and support on all aspects of lesbian and gay parenting.

Relate
www.relate.org.uk
Provides family counselling and family education. Counsellors work in locations throughout England, Wales and Northern Ireland.

The Trust for the Study of Adolescence
www.tsa.uk.com
Promotes the study of adolescence by fostering and stimulating research, disseminating information and raising awareness of the needs of young people.

FOR YOUNG PEOPLE

Child Line
www.childline.org.uk
Children and young people in trouble or in danger can call free on **0800 1111** to talk about any problem. Also produces leaflets and information on child-related issues.

Connexions
www.connexions-direct.com
A comprehensive site for young people, covering issues such as Learning, Finance, Relationships Work and Health. There is a confidential help line Tel: 080 800 13 2 19

TheSite
www.thesite.org
A site for young people which offers advice, information and support on sex, relationships, drugs, drink, health, well-being and money.

HEALTH AND WELL BEING

www.vegsoc.org
The vegetarian society is an educational charity promoting understanding and respect for vegetarian lifestyles.

www.vegansociety.com
for information about a vegan lifestyle.

MENTAL HEALTH, DEPRESSION AND ANXIETY

Samaritans
Confidential emotional support to anyone who is suicidal or despairing. Call 08457 90 90 90 (UK) or 1850 60 90 90 (Eire).

Young Minds
www.youngminds.org.uk
UK national charity committed to improving the mental health of children and young people. Online advice for both parents and young people on various types of emotional distress.

EATING DISORDERS.

www.b-eat.co.uk
Information and help on all aspects of eating disorders, including Anorexia Nervosa, Bulimia Nervosa, binge eating disorder and related eating disorders. Helpline 0845 634 1414 Youthline 0845 634 7659

SINGLE PARENTS STEP FAMILIES

National Council for One Parent Families
www.oneparentfamilies.org.uk
Works to promote the welfare of lone parents and their children. Runs a lone parent helpline and provides a range of information. Campaigns and lobbies on lone parent issues.

SELF HARM

www.selfharm.org.uk
Provides information to help young people cope and recover. Explains different types of self-harm, how common it is, why it is difficult to ask for help.

INTERNET SAFETY

www.direct.gov.uk and search for *Staying Safe Online for Kids*. Other areas of online safety are covered including identity theft, protecting belongings and protecting self.

www.thinkuknow.co.uk
Run by the Child Exploitation and Online Protection (CEOP) Centre. The aim of the website is to help parents and young people understand the potential dangers of new technology. The website has a reporting function which allows users to report abuse and potential abuse online.

www.chatdanger.com
Site for teens looking at the potential dangers from interactive services like IM, online games, emails, internet chat room and mobile phones.

www.netnanny.com
Commercial software providing protection not only for the World Wide Web but also parts of the Internet like the Usenet, Peer-to-Peer downloading networks, Chat Rooms, Instant Messages, FTP, Forums and email.

SUBSTANCE ABUSE

Drugs:

www.talktofrank.com
Useful website for both parents and teenagers worried about drugs and alcohol abuse.

Alcohol:

Al-Anon
www.al-anonuk.org.uk
Offers support specifically to families of people who have a problem with alcohol and drugs

TheSite
www.thesite.org/drinkanddrugs
Owned and run by YouthNet UK, a registered charity, aims to be the first place all young adults turn to when they need support and guidance through life.

Drinkline
free, confidential helpline
0800 917 8282

Smoking:

ASH
www.ash.org.uk
Anti-smoking charity, working to tackle the epidemic of tobacco-related disease. Offers help on giving up.

QUIT
www.quit.org.uk
An independent charity with a free helpline for anyone wanting to quit smoking. Its website has a special section for teens
www.quitbecause.org.uk
There is a also a Free helpline 0800 00 22 00 and free individual same day advice by email
stopsmoking@quit.org.uk

SEXUAL HEALTH

Genitourinary medicine (GUM) clinics are available at most large hospitals

Helplines:
NHS Direct 0845 46 47
NHS 24 (Scotland) 08454 24 24 24
FPA (formerly the Family Planning Association) 0845 310 1334
Sexual Health Line 0800 567 123

Websites
www.brook.org.uk
www.ruthinking.co.uk
www.malehealth.co.uk
Terrence Higgins Trust **www.tht.org.uk**

GETTING INVOLVED

British Trust for Conservation Volunteers
www2.btcv.org.uk
UK organisation promoting practical conservation work by volunteers, BTCV runs thousands of practical conservation projects every year.

Friends of the Earth
www.foe.co.uk
One of the leading environmental pressure groups in the UK.

Greenpeace
www.greenpeace.org
Environmental organisation with campaigns ranging from promoting solutions, to direct action, political lobbying and research.

LAW

Children's Legal Centre
Independent UK charity founded in 1991, concerned with law and policy affecting children and young people.

National Association of Citizens' Advice Bureaux
Advice and information on your legal rights from NACAB.

Victim Support
www.victimsupport.org.uk/vs_england_wales/index.php
Independent UK charity for people affected by crime, offering a free and confidential service, irrespective of whether or not a crime has been reported.

BULLYING

Bullying Online
www.bullying.co.uk
Registered charity providing on-line problem pages plus practical and legal help. Anti-bullying website, tacking the problem at school and (for teenagers) in the workplace.

Bullying: Anti-Bullying Network (Scotland)
Forum for teachers, parents and young people sharing ideas about how bullying should be tackled.

Kidscape
www.kidscape.org.uk
National children's charity focusing on preventative policies with practical, easy to use material for children, parents and teachers.

DfES Don't Suffer In Silence
Packed with new ideas, practical techniques and the valuable experiences of those who have been bullied, or have even bullied others.

HELP

Rape and Sexual Abuse Support Centre
Free, confidential and non-judgemental help and support. Helpline 0208 239 1122 Mon-Friday 12-2.30pm & 7-9.30pm Weekends/public holidays 2.30-5pm.

Victim Support
Independent UK charity for people affected by crime, offering a free and confidential service, irrespective of whether or not a crime has been reported.

EDUCATION

Department for Education and Skills
www.dfes.gov.uk
Government website on all matters to do with education from nursery school to University.

Advisory Centre for Education
News and information for parents, school governors and teachers. Including schools admissions and appeals. **www.ace-ed.org.uk** Freephone adviceline on many subjects like exclusion from school, bullying, special educational needs and school admission appeals. Freephone: 0808 800 5793

After 16
www.after16.org.uk
Aimed at teenagers and young people in the UK who have an impairment or disability and are wondering what opportunities and services there should be when they leave school.

Independent Schools Information Service
www.isc.co.uk
Official site for the 1,300 UK schools accredited by the Independent Schools Council.

Learn Direct
www.learndirect.co.uk
Learn Direct has been developed by Ufi (University for industry) with a remit from government to provide high quality post-16 learning.

GRANTS FOR EDUCATION

www.egas-online.org.uk/fwa/index.html
EGAS operates nationally providing comprehensive advice and information on sources of funding available for post-16 education and training; including loans, grants, benefits, access funds, hardship funds, bursaries and charitable trusts.

www.scholarship-search.org.uk
A comprehensive guide to everything you need when planning and organising your student finances.

PERSONAL SAFETY

www.direct.gov.uk
Other areas of online safety are covered including identity theft, protecting belongings and protecting self.

GAP YEAR TRAVEL

www.immunisation.org.uk
www.fitfortravel.nhs.uk

For information about the necessary injections required for travel to countries outside Europe and the US.

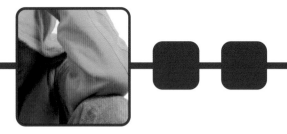

Further reading

General:

How To Talk So Teens Will Listen And Listen So Teens Will Talk
Adele Faber & Elaine Mazlish:
(Useful book on how to communicate with children and young people)

Your Guide to a Happier Family.
Adele Faber & Elaine Mazlish:
(Particularly good on how to praise and avoid labelling young people)

Whatever! A Down-to-Earth Guide to Parenting Teenagers
Gill Hines & Alison Baverstock

What Worries Parents
Kristina Murrin & Paul

The Parentalk Guide to Brothers and Sisters
Pat Spungin & Victoria Richardson

The Teenage Years: Understanding 12-14 Year-Olds
Margot Wadell of The Tavistock Clinic

The Teenager Years: Understanding 15-17 Year-Olds
John Bradley & Helene Dubinsky of The Tavistock Clinic

Enjoy Your Teenagers
Jean Robb & Hilary Letts

Happy Children Through Positive Parenting
Elizabeth Hartley-Brewer

Liberated Parents, Liberated Children
Adele Faber & Elaine Mazlish

How to Talk So Teens Will Listen and Listen So Teens Will Talk
by Adele Faber & Elaine Mazlish

Step Families:
Your Kids, My Kids
Suzie Hayman:
(Step families and how to cope with blending families)

Step by Step Parenting; A Guide to Successful Living with a blended Family
James Echler:
(Very thorough coverage of all emotional issues in the lives of step families).

Issues:
Drugs: A Parent's Guide
Judy Mackie:
(A down to earth guide for parents).

Bullying: a Parent's Guide
Jennifer Thomson
(Ways to find out if your child is being bullied, ways to stop it and build self esteem).

RUBn Bullied? Tips for Teens
Ann Fslynn & Pat Courtney

Let's Talk Sex
Davina McCall & Anita Naik
(Companion to the Channel 4 programme).

The Sex Book
Jane Pavanel

Credits

Author:	Dr Pat Spungin
Project Manager:	Louise McIntyre
Design/page build:	James Robertson
Copy editor:	Ian Heath
Photography:	All photos from istock.com, except for Alamy – alamy.com (pages 53, 131, 132, 133 and 135) and John Birdsall – johnbirdsall.co.uk (pages 5, 8, 18, 39, 46, 49, 116, 123, 138, 139, 143 and 146)